BREAKING FREE OF CHILD ANXIETY AND OCD

BREAKING FREE OF CHILD ANXIETY AND OCD

A Scientifically Proven Program for Parents

ELI R. LEBOWITZ

OXFORD
UNIVERSITY PRESS

OXFORD
UNIVERSITY PRESS

Oxford University Press is a department of the University of Oxford. It furthers the University's objective of excellence in research, scholarship, and education by publishing worldwide. Oxford is a registered trade mark of Oxford University Press in the UK and certain other countries.

Published in the United States of America by Oxford University Press
198 Madison Avenue, New York, NY 10016, United States of America.

© Oxford University Press 2021

Library of Congress Cataloging-in-Publication Data
Names: Lebowitz, Eli R., author.
Title: Breaking free of child anxiety and OCD : a scientifically proven program for parents / Eli R. Lebowitz.
Description: New York, NY : Oxford University Press, 2021. |
Includes bibliographical references and index.
Identifiers: LCCN 2020016659 (print) | LCCN 2020016660 (ebook) |
ISBN 9780190883522 (paperback) | ISBN 9780190883546 (epub)
Subjects: LCSH: Anxiety in children—Treatment—Popular works. |
Obsessive-compulsive disorder in children—Treatment—Popular works. |
Child rearing—Popular works.
Classification: LCC RJ506.A58 L43 2021 (print) | LCC RJ506.A58 (ebook) |
DDC 618.9285/227—dc23
LC record available at https://lccn.loc.gov/2020016659
LC ebook record available at https://lccn.loc.gov/2020016660

9 8 7

Printed by Marquis Book Printing, Canada

Contents

Foreword

"My Child Is Struggling with Anxiety, Can You Help?"

This is a question I get asked very frequently by parents of children and adolescents coping with elevated anxiety. This book answers that question by saying, "*YOU can help your child!*" If you are the parent of a child with anxiety or obsessive-compulsive problems, it is my hope that by following the steps described in these pages, you will be able to significantly reduce your child's anxiety and improve their quality of life.

The steps laid out in this book are a systematic treatment approach that has been tested in clinical trials and found to be very effective. The name of the treatment program is SPACE, which stands for Supportive Parenting for Anxious Childhood Emotions. What many parents find most exciting about SPACE, and what makes it most different from other child anxiety treatments, is that it focuses entirely on parents and provides them with the tools to help their children. In fact, here's a promise: At no point in this book will parents be required to pressure their children into doing things they don't want to do. In working through this book, you'll only be trying to change the behavior of the one person you can control the most, yourself.

Before going any further let's do away with a common myth about childhood problems; namely, that childhood problems are caused by parents, and if your child has an anxiety problem this is probably due to something you did wrong, or to something you should have done but did not. In Chapter 3, I address this myth and explain why it is simply not the case. *The desire to help your children live the best lives they can live, and to overcome challenges they face, is completely separate from the notion that you as a parent caused your child's difficulties.* Once you think about it this way, it becomes obvious that the two things differ. After all, why would a parent only want to help a child with problems the parent had caused? It makes no sense! Likewise, the fact (and it is a fact) that parents can be helpful to their anxious children does not mean that the parents caused the anxiety. Why should parents only be able to impact problems they caused? That also makes no sense. So whether you blame yourself for your child's anxiety, or somebody else blames you for it, or you think that I blame you for it by suggesting you have the power to help your child, let's do away with the myth that you are the cause of your child's anxiety.

Like many other treatments, SPACE is a systematic program in which each step builds on previous steps in an organized way. For this reason, the best way to use this book is to read through the whole book and follow the suggestions in the order they are presented. It can be tempting to jump ahead or skip over steps, especially as you are probably eager to get going and see your child's anxiety improve as soon as possible. But you and your child are most likely to have the best success if you follow each step in order. Taking the time to complete all the steps, and making use of the accompanying worksheets, is really the best way to accomplish your goal of helping your child be less anxious.

Although working through each step takes time, it's useful to remember that treating childhood anxiety always takes time and effort. SPACE has been found to be an effective way of reducing anxiety in children, but this research has focused on clinical studies in which parents attend regular meetings with a skilled therapist every week for around 12 weeks. Other treatments, such as child-based cognitive behavioral therapy (see Chapter 2 for a brief description of CBT), also rely on regular weekly meetings with a therapist and require a lot of work both in the sessions and between them. So don't shortchange yourself when working independently with a book such as this one. Put in the effort and devote the time so that you can be sure you are giving yourself the best chance of success. One suggestion is to commit to your own "session time," setting aside an hour a week, which you (and your partner when working together) will devote to working on this book and thinking about the progress you are making.

Of course, even with substantial time and effort, working with a book can't completely substitute for skilled therapy from an expert clinician. This book contains tools and suggestions that will likely be sufficient for many parents to have a meaningful impact on their child's anxiety. But if you realize that the book is not enough, or if you find that you need more help, then working together with a professional mental health provider who is knowledgeable about child anxiety and experienced in treating it may be the best option.

And finally, thank you! Thank you for being a parent who is sensitive to your child's needs and devoted to helping your child. You are holding a book that is written for parents who want to help their child. Your sensitivity has helped you understand that your child is coping with anxiety, and your dedication has led you to seek out ways to help them. So, thank you!

1

Understanding Child Anxiety

What Is Anxiety?

Anxiety is a word we use to describe the system that helps us become aware of possible threats and dangers and keeps us safe from those threats and dangers. All living things, from the simplest life forms to complex animals and human beings, have systems whose job it is to tell the difference between things that are safe and things that might be harmful. Being able to make this distinction is critical to staying alive and healthy. Some animals use their sense of smell to determine whether a food is safe to eat, whereas others listen to the sounds around them to decide it is safe to leave a protected spot.

We human beings also use our senses to keep out of trouble, such as when we jump at a loud noise, look both ways before we cross the street, or sniff a yogurt container to decide whether it smells good enough to eat. Human beings also can react to threats that are not actually present and that cannot be detected by our senses. Our unique ability to *imagine* dangers, and take steps to avoid them, is a tremendously important human asset. We can prevent a dangerous encounter before it happens, and the ability to do so relies on our imagination. After all, if a threat is not yet present in the real world, then the only place it can exist for us is in our imagination.

When we imagine something bad or dangerous happening, the imaginary scenario can activate our anxiety system, just as if the bad thing were happening in real life. Imagine getting a call from your doctor, who tells you that your recent test results are worrying and that she wants you to come in to the office as soon as possible, preferably that same day, to discuss the results and do more tests. Try to imagine this vividly and really hear the concern and urgency in your doctor's voice. How does this make you feel? Perhaps scared or worried and maybe your body feels a little more tense than it did a moment ago. Perhaps you want to stop these imaginary fears, cut them short, and remind yourself that they are not real.

Feeling this way is a completely normal reaction and this is an example of just how wonderful a thing our imagination is. Thinking about negative or dangerous scenarios is one of the most important things that our imagination does. Of course, we usually prefer to spend our daydreaming time thinking up pleasant things that we wish *would* happen, and that, too, is an important function of imagination. But thinking of all the bad things that can happen is more useful for staying safe. Our imaginations may even have evolved specifically to allow us to think about risks and dangers rather than fun, pleasant things.

Take another example. Imagine that an acquaintance asks you to invest money in a new scheme he has for making big money fast. You might think about:

- How nice it would be to turn a little money into a lot.
- How great it would feel to solve your financial challenges once and for all.
- How proud you would be telling friends and family that you grasped the financial opportunity of a lifetime.

But you might have some other thoughts as well:

- You might feel skeptical and imagine losing your hard-earned cash on a wacky scheme.
- You might imagine how embarrassing it would be to tell people that you squandered your income on a fly-by-night idea.

If you only had the first kind of thoughts—the pleasant scenarios where you get rich easily—you would probably jump on the chance to invest as much as possible. The negative thoughts—less pleasant but critically important—may protect you from an impulsive or reckless course of action that could spell disaster. By conjuring negative outcomes and triggering your anxiety about those outcomes as though they were actually happening, your imagination can keep you safe from dangers in the real world.

Being able to respond to imaginary threats before they occur comes at a price. When we open ourselves to anxiety about imaginary dangers, we become vulnerable to worries that actually are not realistic or likely at all. Asking "what if" questions—the constant refrain of the anxious mind—means we can come up with some pretty unrealistic "what ifs." Responding to made-up scenarios with very real anxiety means that we can be genuinely anxious about many things that don't pose a threat at all. We can even be scared of things we know don't exist, such as ghosts and witches.

Making wise decisions requires that we consider a wide variety of possible imaginary scenarios and then come up with a way to evaluate them so that the most realistic and likely ones carry more weight than the highly unlikely or outlandish ones. We also need to balance the possible risks against the potential benefits of various courses of action. Getting rich fast might be very nice, but is it nice enough to justify the risk of losing the money we already have? Making these kinds of wise decisions relies on two skills that humans are not always good at:

- We need to be able to figure out which scenarios are the more likely ones and which are more improbable.
- We need to be able to assign values to just how good or bad possible outcomes would be.

These are both really difficult things to do, especially when the currently available information is quite limited. Remember, we are dealing with imaginary scenarios, so real-life information is not always available.

Different people approach this challenge in different ways. For example, are you the kind of person who would rather play it safe, or are you more of a risk taker? If you prefer to play it safe, this probably means you are giving more weight to the negative scenarios in your mind than to the positive ones. If you are a risk taker, you may be more open to believing that potential positive outcomes are the most likely. Or it might be that you place higher value on positive outcomes than on negative ones.

If you are reading this book, it is likely that you are the parent of a child or adolescent, and that you have some concern about your child's anxiety levels. Try thinking about your child's anxiety in terms of the way she reacts to imaginary scenarios in her own mind:

- Does she seem to always come up with the worst scenarios imaginable?
- Have you ever felt frustrated that she "chooses" to focus on the negative rather than the positive?
- Does your child seem to downplay the possibility that things will actually go well, and "choose" to believe that they won't?
- Perhaps even when things turn out fine and the negative event your child feared does not happen, does it seem as if she "refuses" to learn from this, or to believe that it could go this way again?

I put the words "choose" and "refuses" in quotes because these are probably not the right words to use. Children don't actually get to choose whether to believe in the negative or positive scenarios that they imagine. Of course, adults don't get that choice either, but when you are the parent of a child with anxiety, it can seem like the child stubbornly sticks to his anxious statements, behaviors, or beliefs. If you believe that your child can choose to just turn off his anxiety and be less worried, you may be feeling exasperated, which can lead you to become angry or annoyed with your child. It is important to understand, however, that human brains function in different ways, and some children are going to be more anxious than others, whether they want to be or not. This can be a good thing when it keeps them safe and out of trouble. But it can be a liability by making them more vulnerable to avoiding things that are not actually dangerous.

Think back to the two skills needed to make rational decisions that balance risk and reward: (1) the ability to estimate the probability of different events and (2) the ability to ascribe values of *how good* or *how bad* these outcomes would be if they occurred. Table 1.1 provides examples of what I mean by "ascribing values," both positive and negative. When we say that a child is anxious, we usually are describing a child who shows some predictable patterns in how he uses each of these abilities. A child who is anxious is typically going to *overestimate the likelihood of negative events,* and to *downplay the likelihood of positive ones.* An anxious child also is probably going to *view negative events as extremely negative (having high value),* more so than might seem reasonable to a less anxious person. On the other hand, an anxious child often will *view positive events as less positive (having a low value),* making those potential good outcomes less likely to influence his decision-making. What is the ultimate outcome of these predictable patterns of thinking? *If negative events seem*

TABLE 1.1. Examples of Ascribing Positive and Negative Values to Events

	Positive	*Negative*
High Value	This is going to be the best trip ever!	This trip is going to be a nightmare!
Low Value	This trip is going to be fine.	This trip will probably be boring.

highly probable and very high-value, while positive events seem less likely and not that positive anyway, it is not surprising that anxious children tend to veer away from risk taking and move toward a more cautious course of action.

One more thing contributes to making this predictable pattern even more powerful. Anxious children are *really good at coming up with those negative events* and often imagine outcomes that would not occur to someone else. Where one child might be able to come up with one or two relatively obvious negative outcomes, an anxious child's imagination might summon many.

Consider a child who is thinking about having a birthday party and is wondering whether to go ahead with the plan. Many different scenarios might go through her mind, some positive and some negative. She may imagine becoming more popular as everyone has a great time at her house. She may envision receiving nice gifts from her friends. She may think about having fun and spending a great afternoon together with other children. On the other hand, the birthday child might think about negative possibilities, such as many kids choosing not to attend. Or she might imagine the party being a dud and guests saying they did not have fun. She might imagine that something embarrassing will happen at the party, leaving her feeling humiliated and ashamed to go back to school. Or perhaps she imagines other children talking about her and saying something mean or unfriendly.

For anxious children, the second set of scenarios, in which things go badly and they end up regretting having the party in the first place, might seem considerably more likely and compelling. The high value of the negative events ("it would be terrible," or "a disaster," or "the end of the world") might outweigh the potential positives, to which they have given a lower value ("it would be fine" or "OK"). Anxious children might also come up with negative scenarios that would not have occurred to less anxious children, such as a storm or a fire ruining the party, someone drowning in the pool, everyone getting food poisoning from the cake, or the birthday child throwing up in front of all the guests.

If your child is anxious, he cannot simply choose to ignore all these negative possibilities, or decide to believe that only the positive ones will occur. Neither can he decide that the negative events wouldn't be all that terrible. It is easy to see why a child prone to higher levels of anxiety is likely to decide to skip the party altogether; the risk does not seem worth it. Hosting a party and taking on that level of risk might feel to an anxious child as reckless and foolhardy as investing all your money in a get-rich-quick scheme.

Why Do Some Children Struggle with Anxiety?

Common questions asked by parents of children with anxiety include:

- *Why is this happening?*
- *How come other children don't have this problem?*
- *Is it because he's a middle child?*
- *Was it something we did?*
- *Is it in her DNA?*

If your child seems to struggle with anxiety more than other children, you may be wondering why? The science of mental health does not have a good answer as to why some children are more anxious than others. It may seem surprising that we don't yet have good solid answers to such an important question. But if you consider two things, you'll realize that it's actually not that surprising:

- The first thing is that psychology and psychiatry—the disciplines that focus on mental health and emotional wellbeing—are relatively new fields of medicine. There have always been children and adults struggling with anxiety, but studying these problems scientifically, as part of the broader field of medicine, is relatively new.

- The second thing to realize is just how complicated and challenging the human brain is, and how limited are the tools we have to study it. A human brain has tens of billions of neurons, interconnected through a web of synapses and is far more complex than the most sophisticated machinery. Understanding how the brain functions normally, at the most rudimentary level, is a tremendously challenging task that is still very much ongoing. The tools we have to study the brain are also extremely limited.

Considering the complexity of the brain, the limited tools available for studying it, and the relatively brief time it has been studied, science has provided a lot of valuable information about anxiety and other problems. But there is not yet a clear answer as to why one child struggles with high levels of anxiety, while another does not. And there is not likely to be one answer to that question. Multiple things can contribute to a child's anxiety level, including internal and biological factors as well as external and environmental factors. It appears that some children are born with the tendency to be more anxious, through a combination of genetically inherited and randomly determined features of their DNA, which is the genetic code that determines the characteristics of living things. Even simple characteristics such as eye color, long thought to be determined by a single gene, have turned out to be more complex than scientists previously believed, and there is no single "gene for anxiety."

Environmental factors, starting with the prenatal environment and continuing with the child's environment after birth, may also play a role. In most cases, the environment may be influencing biological and genetic factors that were already there.

Sometimes, it is tempting to assume that a certain environmental factor is the cause of a child's anxiety. Both parents and therapists may fall into this trap. For example, if a child is adopted, or parents get divorced or frequently argue, or the child has been bullied in school, or is gifted academically, or has a chronic illness, or is overweight, or has lost a loved one, it is natural to assume that this is the cause of the anxiety problem. Of course, it may be that these issues have contributed to the child being anxious, or such factors may be the thing the child is anxious about. But it is not necessarily the case that without this factor, this particular child would not have been anxious. It is quite possible that the child is anxious for unknown or unknowable reasons, and that these known factors are just serving as "hooks" on which to hang an explanation for something that defies explanation. Of course, anything that can be done to provide children with a healthy and stable environment should be done, but it is wrong to assume that a child's anxiety problem is the result of a particular feature of his life.

So what can be done? There are effective ways of overcoming anxiety that do not rely on knowing *why* a child has an anxiety problem. Even in other areas of medicine, there are many treatments that are used because they work and not because doctors understand exactly why someone has the problem. This book focuses mainly on one method of reducing anxiety through changes you can make to your own behavior as a parent. In the next chapter you'll read about additional approaches, and I encourage you to consider the various options to get as much as help as possible for your child.

How Common Are Anxiety Problems?

Anxiety problems are the most common mental health problems in children and adolescents. More specifically, studies indicate that between 5% and 10% of children from preschool through adolescence have a current anxiety problem. Taking the midpoint of 7.5% (which is very close to what has recently been reported in one large-scale study), this means that in a typical classroom with 25 children, two students are expected to have an anxiety problem *at any given time*. If your child has an anxiety problem, she is probably not the only one! And the number is much higher if we ask how many children *will ever* have an anxiety problem, rather than how many have one right now. Data suggest that as many as one in three children will have an anxiety problem at some point before the end of adolescence.

These are very high numbers and raise questions such as: Why is anxiety so prevalent? Is the prevalence rising? And what should be done about it? It may be that certain aspects of living in today's world, such as the immersion in social media, or a tendency toward more achievement and evaluation, cause children to be more anxious. But it is likely that most of the children who are anxious today would have struggled with anxiety in other times as well, and that we are simply more aware of child anxiety and more likely to detect it than we were in the past.

Anxiety Problem or Anxiety Disorder?

Throughout this book, I prefer to describe children as having "anxiety problems" or being "highly anxious" rather than as having an "anxiety disorder." There are a number of reasons for this choice, but you may replace the term with one you prefer and the meaning will not change. One reason to avoid the more clinical "anxiety disorder" is that a child does not have to have an actual *disorder* for the tools and strategies described in this book to be helpful. Even if your child is only a little bit anxious, and would not meet formal diagnostic criteria for an anxiety disorder, you can still help him to cope better and be less anxious. In fact, helping your child who has only a moderate (or "subclinical") level of anxiety may be particularly important, because it may help him not to reach the anxiety level that would qualify for a formal diagnosis.

Another reason not to focus on formal diagnoses and disorders is that these diagnoses are actually quite arbitrary, and the decision as to whether a child has an anxiety disorder is ultimately subjective. Because there is no blood test or X-ray to determine the presence of an anxiety disorder, that decision rests on whether the child or their parents believe that anxiety is interfering with the child's life in a meaningful way. If you are reading this book, you probably feel that anxiety is a significant factor in making your child less happy or less able to function as you would expect. In that case, the strategies in this book are probably relevant for you regardless of formal diagnosis.

Yet another reason to focus on anxiety problems as opposed to disorders is that anxiety disorders are highly "comorbid," that is, if a child has one anxiety disorder, it is likely she also has at least one other anxiety disorder. Mental health professionals classify anxiety disorders into specific and separate diagnoses based on the main "triggers" for the anxiety (e.g., is your child afraid of cats or of social situations?) and based on the main ways in which the anxiety is expressed (e.g., is your child primarily a worrier, or do they become acutely physically anxious?). These separate categories are useful for some purposes, but they are not completely distinct entities, and a child who is anxious about both cats and social situations may simply be a highly anxious child whose anxiety shows up in multiple situations.

Finally, the term "disorder" can be confusing because it can seem to suggest an *explanation* for a problem, rather than merely *describing* the problem. Knowing that your child has an anxiety disorder means that the level of anxiety-related interference she experiences is high enough to warrant clinical attention, and learning more about the disorder can help you better understand your child. For example, you may learn that certain behaviors you did not link to anxiety are actually symptoms of the anxiety disorder. But knowing that your child has an anxiety disorder is not an explanation for why he is anxious, it is simply an acknowledgment that he is.

What Does Anxiety Look Like?

Anxiety shows itself in many ways. For example,

- *She can't fall asleep at night; her mind just seems to be stuck in* ع *overdrive.* ७
- *He won't try anything new—he'd rather do the same thing every* ७ *single day.*
- *She overreacts to everything.* ७
- *He can't stand it when we don't have a detailed plan for the day.* ع
- *She can never make up her mind, she just hates making decisions.* ع
- *He just seems grumpy all the time.*
- *He'll fly into a panic at the slightest thing.* ७
- *She says she wants friends, but she ignores anyone who tries to get close to her.*
- *He's always thinking 10 steps ahead into the future.* ع

Anxiety can look very different for different children. It's useful to think about a child's functioning in four separate domains, and how anxiety can impact each domain in different ways. The four domains are: *body, thoughts, behaviors,* and *feelings.* Your child's anxiety is likely impacting all four of these domains to some degree, but for some children one domain is going to be the most clearly affected, while for other children it will be a different domain. For example, you may recognize mostly the changes in your child's thoughts and behaviors, and not notice as many changes in his body or feelings. Or your child may seem most anxious in her body, and not as much in the other domains. As you read about the various domains, think about how each applies to your child, and use Worksheet 1 (How Is Anxiety Impacting Your Child?) in Appendix A at the end of this book, to write down the ways anxiety is impacting your child.

Body

The body category refers to all the things that make up your child's physical experience, even the things her body does without her noticing. When a child is anxious, her physical functioning can change quite a bit, and over time being frequently anxious can lead to longer term changes in her body. Think about what your child's body is like when she is anxious. Her muscles might seem more stiff, taut, or rigid. Her breathing might speed up or become more shallow. Some children will tremble when they are anxious, or they may feel sensations such as lightheadedness or nausea. Their stomachs can feel different, for example, they may feel crampy, achy, or upset. Some children will notice that they are sweating more because of anxiety, or that their mouths are dry. They may complain of various other physical sensations, such as just feeling weird or strange or as though their hearts are pounding. There also can be changes in the body that your child does not notice. You may notice some of these, such as increased fidgeting or twitching, but some changes are probably not noticeable at all, such as dilating pupils or changes in body temperature.

These changes in the body are normal when we are feeling anxious, and they make up part of the short-term "flight or fight response" that evolved to help humans cope with dangerous situations. The body is reacting to the sense of danger by gearing up for a fight or an escape. But when your child is not able to do those things, either because there is no actual danger present or because flight and fight are not appropriate actions, she gets stuck with those feelings and the experience can be very unpleasant. In fact, if your child is anxious much of the time, the repeated activation of the fight or flight response can take a toll. She may start to complain of more aches and pains, such as headache, backache, or stomachache. Anxiety also makes it harder to get sleep and rest, and the loss of relaxing downtime can have a negative impact on mood, concentration, and overall health.

It's important to know that those short-term physical feelings of anxiety are not dangerous in a healthy child. Pounding heart and shortness of breath can be frightening for you as well as for your child, but it is just your child's body doing what it is meant to do when he is feeling scared. Your child's body works just as hard when he goes for a quick run, plays a ball game, or is being wild with his siblings, as it does when he is anxious. The feelings are not as frightening when running or playing because you both know why your child's body is all worked up, but he is just as safe when the cause is anxiety. And just like after your child stops running or being wild, following a period of anxiety his body will slowly wind down and return to a state of normal activity, with slower heart rate and deeper breathing. Feeling scared also can quickly drive your child's body into overdrive, but give it time and it will wind back down. Learning that the body knows how to calm itself, even without doing anything special, is very reassuring. Even if your child does not know how to calm himself, and even if you are not able to do it for him, his body will do it on its own if you give it some time.

Thoughts

How we are feeling has a strong effect on how we see and think about the world around us. Earlier in this chapter you read about ways that anxious children's thoughts are different from the thoughts of children who are less anxious. Anxious children (1) tend to be very good at coming up with negative scenarios in their imagination, (2) tend to assign high values to those negative possibilities, making them seem even worse than they might appear to another child, and (3) tend to perceive negative events as more likely to happen than is realistically true. Even people who are not usually anxious tend to overestimate the likelihood of negative events occurring when they are feeling anxious. Interestingly, it's not just the thing that makes us anxious that seems more likely to happen; *all negative events* seem more likely when we're feeling anxious. This is one reason why worries seem to stick so easily to anxious children.

Another thing you may have noticed in your anxious child's thoughts is how focused she can become on her anxiety, even at the expense of being able to pay attention to other things. Sometimes it can seem as though she doesn't want to talk about anything else! If you put yourself in your child's shoes, however, it becomes easy to see why this happens. Human brains developed to consider threats first and everything else later. When we have detected a threat, it makes sense to put other things on hold until the threat has been dealt with. Imagine if you were on the phone with a colleague, talking about an important issue relating to work, while also trying to cook dinner. What would happen if you accidentally started a little fire in your kitchen because of some hot oil? You would probably drop the phone and focus on putting out the fire! Isn't the conversation about work important? Of course it is, but it's going to have to wait. Your brain has to make a choice about what to prioritize *right now* and, as they say, safety first! Now think about what it's like to be in your child's head. If he goes through the day feeling like there's a fire that has to be put out, then everything else is going to take a back seat. It makes no sense to focus on what a teacher is saying, for example, if your brain is feeling as though there's a fire in the classroom. When you actually have a fire in your kitchen, you can take action to put it out, and then you can go back to thinking about other things like your work call. But when your child is feeling anxious, there may not be any action he can take to put out the fire because the fire exists only in his mind. The results are that your child may seem as if he has tunnel vision, and is narrowly focused and stuck on thinking about his anxiety or worries.

It's not only the kind of thoughts we have word for word in our heads that are impacted by anxiety. How we allocate attention, second by second and even faster, is also affected by anxiety. Psychologists call the tendency to pay more attention to anxiety-provoking things "attention-bias," and anxious children tend to have this kind of bias. Our brains are constantly flooded with sights, sounds, and smells from the world around us—so much so that it is impossible for the human brain to pay equal attention to everything our senses detect. We just can't do it, and so our brains are constantly making choices. Imagine having an assistant whose job it is to go through your mail and screen out unimportant things so that you can focus on the few things that matter. The assistant is helping you to keep a narrow focus by choosing only a small portion of all the letters and junk mail.

Or imagine walking into a room. You'll probably notice certain things, such as seeing other people or smelling a strong odor. If you are particularly observant, you may notice the color of the walls, the number of chairs, or the pattern on the carpet. But there are probably many things you *won't* notice, and, interestingly, the things that you *do* notice are not random. For example, most people walking into a room will notice whether or not somebody else is there, but only a much smaller number of people would be able to say whether the window was open or closed. If you saw a weapon in the room, you would certainly notice that, because your brain would want you to be aware of something that might be dangerous. It's as though your assistant were going through the mail and found a suspicious letter. He would definitely want to bring that to your attention before anything else.

Your child's brain is also constantly making choices about what to notice and what not to pay attention to. And those choices are also not random. If your child is highly anxious they are probably going to pay more attention to things that make them anxious than to things that seem neutral or safe. And because more things seem threatening to them they are going to be busy with those, and less free to pay attention to other stuff. It's as though your child's secretary was misinterpreting innocent letters as death threats, and constantly rushing in to let your child know about some new danger, interrupting everything else. Psychological studies have shown that anxious children show attention-bias toward threat even faster than the conscious mind can process information. Show an anxious child two pictures, a neutral one and a scary one for even half a second, not enough time for them to actually process the pictures consciously, and their attention will already be captivated by the scary picture, making them less likely to attend to the other one.

Have you ever had a thought that just came into your head, without you wanting to think about it? Have you ever tried to stop thinking about something, but the thought kept coming anyway? Realizing that we can have thoughts that are not intentional, and therefore don't represent us, is a useful insight for understanding an anxious child. Your anxious child may have scary, worrying, or embarrassing thoughts that she doesn't actually want to have. If we take all those thoughts as representing who your child is at some deep level, then it can seem like her brain is a very strange place indeed. But your child is not particularly strange for having these thoughts; we all have brains that are a little bit strange. I bet you would not want someone else to be able to see all the thoughts that go through your mind. You know that you have many thoughts, some are reasonable, rational, and orderly; some are messy, guilty, absurd, and all jumbled up. That's what the human brain is like! Your child may have more anxious thoughts than other children, rather than having different thoughts.

✳We Can't Stop Our Thoughts ✳

Have you tried to tell your child things like "don't think about it," "you don't need to worry about that," or "just stop obsessing over it"? Even if you have not, it's virtually guaranteed that someone has given that kind of advice to your child. And it is equally certain that the advice hasn't helped very much. If your child were able to turn off his anxious thoughts at will, he probably would have done so a long time ago! The truth is that *we don't get to pick what we think*. Our brains are going to serve up lots and lots of thoughts that we would prefer not to have, and there's not all that much we can do about it. In fact, trying to stop yourself from thinking a thought is going to make you more likely to think it. Getting into a fight with your brain, trying to force it not to think something, or attempting to push away a scary thought because it makes you uncomfortable, almost always has the opposite effect.

For some children, a large part of their anxiety problem is getting stuck in endlessly trying to push away an unpleasant or scary thought, and ending up having the thought occur more and more. This can happen with regular worries, such as thoughts about succeeding in school or staying healthy. Your child might get trapped in what seems like an endless cycle of worry and trying not to worry. It can also happen with obsessive thoughts, as in obsessive-compulsive disorder. Obsessions are exactly that, thoughts or feelings that we don't want to have in our heads and that keep coming anyway. A child with obsessions can spend tremendous amounts of time and energy trying to get rid of their undesirable thoughts, and yet always feel as though the thoughts just keep coming, or are even getting worse.

Behavior

Your child's behavior, all the things she does and does not do, are also impacted by anxiety. Remember that it is the job of the anxiety system to keep us safe and away from harm. The main way our anxiety system does this is by causing us to want to avoid things that trigger anxiety. If the anxiety system made us want to do the opposite—to approach the things that trigger anxiety—then it would be doing a very poor job of keeping us out of harm's way! You may have noticed things that your child is unwilling to do because of anxiety, or things she does only with more difficulty than you would expect. A child with a fear of storms, for example, might not want to go outside when the sky is overcast, and a child with a fear of social situations may try to skip school on the day he is due to present in front of the class. That is just his anxiety system saying, "Danger—Keep out!"

Over time, children with anxiety problems tend to gradually increase and broaden the circle of things they avoid. This is also a natural tendency of the anxiety system and a useful one in many situations. For example, if you ate bad food at one branch of a restaurant chain, you might prefer not to visit any of the other branches. If you had an unpleasant encounter with one snake, you might develop a preference for avoiding all snakes. This kind of "avoidance-creep" or *generalization of avoidance* does have some unfortunate side effects. It means that over time your child's anxiety might have an increasingly serious impact on his ability to function in daily life. As your child avoids more and more things, the number of places and situations where he feels safe will get smaller and smaller.

Avoidance has some additional unfortunate side effects. When your child avoids things because of anxiety, there is very little opportunity for him to find out whether those things actually are dangerous. If, for example, your child never goes to school on days with oral presentations, then he won't have many chances to find out whether presentations are really as bad as he imagines. He also won't have opportunities to find out whether he is able to cope with the fear and to tolerate it.

Anxiety and avoidance can cause your child *to do* things, as well as *not* to do them. Take the example of the child who is afraid of storms. Her fear is causing her not to go outside on cloudy days. But the fear also could cause her to do things she would not otherwise do, such as check the weather forecast multiple times throughout the day, or ask an adult whether a storm is coming. Just as with the avoidance (not going out on a cloudy day), the things anxiety causes children to do can interfere with daily life, taking time, energy, and attention away from other things. Like the avoidance, the list of things an anxious child does because of her anxiety can grow longer and longer over time.

Some of the effects of anxiety on behavior may be a little harder to recognize as coming from the anxiety. When a child is avoiding a feared situation, or checking the weather multiple times, it is fairly easy to recognize the behavior as being related to a fear of storms. But other changes in behavior are not quite as obvious. Changes in daily habits may be the effect of anxiety. For example,

- An anxious child may have more difficulty sleeping, wake up more often during the night, or complain of nightmares, and the link to the anxiety may not be obvious at first.

- Changes to a child's eating and appetite also may result from him being overly anxious, including both increased and decreased appetite.
- Anxiety can have an impact on a child's mood, causing him to have more temper outbursts or to fight more with parents or siblings.

If you notice changes like these in your child, they may be related to the anxiety. They may not be, but if such behaviors are not typical of your child and there are other indicators that she is experiencing elevated anxiety, then it is definitely possible that these changes are also anxiety related.

Even when behavioral changes are directly related to a fear or anxiety, the link may be hard to identify at first. A child with separation anxiety may begin to wet his bed, for example, because he is scared of getting up alone during the night. Or he may become uncharacteristically oppositional at bedtime or shower time, because he is scared of being alone in his bed or the bathroom. If you notice changes in your child's behavior, consider the possibility that these are related to anxiety. Try asking your child what is making it harder for him to do these things, and don't assume that he is merely being "naughty" or noncompliant.

Another behavioral change common in anxious children, and one that can frustrate parents no end, is increased clinginess. Throughout this book you will read about how parents frequently become involved in their child's anxiety problem, and about how natural it is for anxious children to want to be near their parents. As a parent, your very presence can have an anxiety-reducing effect on your child, and it is no surprise that children who are anxious find many ways of staying close to their parents. Your child might want to be near you physically, maintaining contact as much as possible, such as holding your hand or sitting in your lap. Or she may want to be interacting with you as much as possible, asking you endless questions, or calling you from the other room for seemingly trivial reasons. Even if you are not in the same place, your child may still want to be in contact with you, through phone calls or text messages. Don't assume that your child is demanding attention for no reason, or is less mature than you expect. You will learn many tools in this book for helping your child to cope better on her own and to take charge of her own anxiety with less help from you. But it's fair to acknowledge that your child is not simply being needy or babyish when her anxiety causes her to seek your closeness more than usual.

Feelings

Anxiety also impacts how a child feels. In fact, anxiety can impact emotion in several different ways. Some of these influences are relatively obvious and straightforward, while others are more subtle and harder to detect. The emotion most closely associated with anxiety, and the one that is easiest to recognize as stemming from it, is fear. When your child is anxious, he may tell you that he feels afraid, or you may see it on his face without him having to tell you. Uncontrolled fear can be an intensely unpleasant emotion to have, and your child is going to want to change his feeling as soon as he can. Many children do enjoy feeling afraid in some situations, such as when they want to watch a scary movie or ride a thrilling roller coaster, but those feelings are enjoyable precisely because the fear is not uncontrolled. When your child picks a scary movie to watch, he is making a choice, and he knows that he can control the situation if he decides he's had enough. In those circumstances even a child who is highly anxious might enjoy feeling afraid. Feeling fear that is not a choice and that is uncontrollable, however, is a very different experience, one that very few people would enjoy.

Almost everyone knows the phrase "fight or flight," but many people overlook the *fight* component of anxiety. Assuming that your child is anxious only when she is cowering in fear can cause you to mislabel fight behaviors as something other than anxiety. Anger, aggression, and even rage are feelings that can promote fight behaviors in response to a threat. If your child has become more irritable, angry, or cranky, or if she has started having more temper tantrums or outbursts of rage, consider the possibility that these changes have more to do with anxiety than with some inherent tendency to misbehave. Psychologists who study child development have found that the link between anxiety and anger can be very strong.

High levels of anxiety don't only increase the frequency of emotions such as fear and anger, they can also lead to a decrease in more positive emotions. A child who is anxious is not going to feel relaxed, calm, or confident; she is also less likely to feel happy, curious, excited, or friendly. When your child is anxious, her brain is in a defensive mode that prioritizes protecting her well-being over other goals. She may seem less generous or sociable, or she may have less interest in the things she normally enjoys. Some of these problems overlap with the symptoms of depression. It is not surprising that so many children with depression also have an anxiety problem, and that many anxious children are also depressed.

Living in a Minefield

Many parents of children who struggle with high levels of anxiety describe their children as rigid, inflexible, and hating change. Thinking about the experience of being an anxious child can help to see why such a child might match these descriptions.

Throughout this book I present examples. Sometimes they describe a specific child or family, but other times, as in the one just below, I present stories or metaphors to help you imagine what the experience of anxiety can be like:

For just a moment, imagine that you've found yourself in a minefield. You need to get out, but you're scared because you know that every step could go BOOM! Think about how you would walk out of the minefield. For one thing you would probably want to take as few steps as possible! No point in taking extra steps when each could be your last. You would focus only on getting out, and you'd ignore anything else that required additional steps. If you saw a beautiful flower a few yards away, you wouldn't go over to look at it. Seeing a pretty flower is nice, but it's definitely not worth the risk of getting blown up by a mine. There's another thing you'd probably realize pretty quickly: If you have to backtrack, it's much better to step only in places where you've already stepped. Any spot you've already stepped is going to be infinitely safer than anyplace new. _New_ means _untried, untested, and potentially catastrophic_, whereas repeating a step means safety and confidence.

Think of your child as living with mines all around him. Your child's anxiety can make him feel that his life is like a minefield, full of the potential for danger and catastrophe. Of course he doesn't want to take extra steps. Doing as little as possible, staying away from dangerous experiences, is just common sense! You may feel frustrated that your child is not willing to try new things or needs everything to always go exactly the same way, but for a child in a minefield, this comes naturally. Your child may be willing to give up on lots of potentially pleasant and fun experiences because of the risk of a very negative experience:

- Could the party be fun? Sure. Will he go? Definitely not! Because it could also be terrible.
- Might a new and unfamiliar food taste good? It might. Will she taste it? No! Because it could taste awful.

Doing something different or taking a risk can feel like wandering over to look at a flower in the middle of a minefield—it just doesn't seem worth it.

A change that seems trivial and unimportant to you can seem risky and dangerous to your child when she's navigating a minefield. If, for example, you have to drive a different route to school, your child may react with high anxiety or anger. You may wonder, what does it matter? And that's precisely the point! Your child doesn't know whether it matters or not and doesn't want to take the risk of finding out. Increasing your child's *flexibility* (the ability to cope with the unexpected) is one of the benefits of lowering her anxiety. But in the meantime, remembering that your child is navigating a minefield of anxiety may help you to be empathetic about rigidity or inflexibility that seem irrational and unnecessary.

Staying in Control

Some other words that parents commonly use to describe anxious children are controlling, bossy, and acting as though the world revolves around them. Once again, considering life from the perspective of an anxious child can help you understand why he may seem that way.

Have you ever gone to an escape room? They're a fun group activity where you have one hour to solve some riddles and puzzles, with each solution taking you one step closer to the key that will open the door and let you out of the room. Of course, you can leave the room at any time because it's just a game, and at the end of an hour you'll leave the room whether you've solved all the puzzles or not. The game is fun precisely because you know it's a game. You know you're not really trapped, and you can enjoy the challenge. If you make a mistake, it doesn't really matter, and if one of your party is not working very hard on the puzzles, well that's his loss.

Now imagine that you're in the same escape room, but one person in your group doesn't realize it's a game. Your instructor said you have one hour to solve everything if you want to get out, and this one person doesn't understand that the instructor was playacting. Your teammate thinks you have an hour to solve all these tricky puzzles and figure out every riddle or you're all going to be trapped in here forever! This doesn't sound like much fun anymore, does it? The riddles and puzzles are exactly the same, but the experience is very different. Your teammate, who thinks the escape is for real, sees every second as precious and every error as a terrifying setback. How is he going to behave? He's probably going to be confused and angry that everyone else isn't taking this seriously enough! He's going think he needs to take control and make sure you're all working as hard as you can, because anybody who isn't trying his or her best is putting everyone's future in jeopardy.

When you feel confident that everything is going to work out, it's easy to let things play out as they will. You don't need to take control because one way or the other, things are going to be fine. But when you feel that danger is all around, and that there is just one way that things might possibly turn out all right, you're going to do everything in your power to make sure they go exactly that way! Having an anxious child in the family is a little bit like being stuck in an escape room with one teammate who doesn't realize it's a game. She is going to be confused by everyone else's lackadaisical and careless manner. She might get angry when others don't seem to be taking things seriously enough. And she is probably going to want to take control to make sure things get done right! It's no surprise that anxious children can seem bossy or controlling. They're fighting for their lives while everyone else is just playing along. It might be irritating and exasperating for you, but it can be infuriating and utterly bewildering for such children. Your child probably knows that her controlling behavior annoys you, but she may also feel as though she has very little choice if she wants to escape the room in time!

In This Chapter You Learned:

- What anxiety is
- Why some children struggle with anxiety
- How common anxiety problems are
- Why this book uses "problem" rather than "disorder"
- How anxiety impacts a child's thoughts, body, feelings, and behavior

2

Child Anxiety

Types and Treatments

What Are the Main Types of Childhood and Adolescent Anxiety?

There is no limit to the variety of things that can cause a child anxiety, but some fears and worries are more common than others, and the most common are classified into various disorders. In this section you'll learn about the commonly diagnosed anxiety disorders. *The important thing to understand, however, is not which label to assign, but how to help your child become less anxious.* Whether or not your child meets the criteria for one or more of these disorders, if she is struggling with high levels of anxiety then you can take steps to help her live a happier and less anxious life. As you read about the anxiety disorders, you may recognize one or more of these labels as a good fit for your child. If you are still unsure about whether your child is anxious, or if you want to know more about the correct diagnosis, then a consultation with a mental health professional may be able to provide answers to your questions.

Separation Anxiety

Separation anxiety is the most common anxiety problem in preadolescent children and can occur in older children as well. Children with separation anxiety will show significant distress at actual separations from primary caregivers, or even at the possibility of being separated. The separation does not have to be long, and some children will be afraid of even the shortest separations. They may be scared to sleep on their own and prefer to sleep in your bed, or have you sleep next to them. If your child has separation anxiety, he may be worried about something bad happening to him when you are not there, or about something happening to you when you're away, or both. In some cases children—especially young children—may not verbalize any particular fear about the separation, and the anxiety may come out through their behavior. Nightmares about separation are common in children with separation anxiety, and such dreams can increase the difficulty with bedtime or lead to other sleep-related problems.

Your child may become agitated when he thinks he is going to be separated from you. He may cry, vomit, yell, tremble, or become angry. He may try to cling to you to avoid separation. School attendance can be challenging because of the prolonged separation, and separation anxiety can lead to absenteeism. If your child is anxious about being separated from you, he may ask you repeated questions about your plans, or ask you to promise that you are not going to leave. He also may try to contact you by phone or text message when you are not together.

Social Anxiety

Social anxiety (also called *social phobia*) is common in young children and adolescents, and tends to start earlier for girls than for boys. Most children with social anxiety are fearful of a variety of social situations, and feel anxious in any situation that they perceive as involving judgment or evaluation, but some children are only afraid of specific situations such as performing in front of an audience.

If your child has social anxiety, she may fear or avoid social situations, especially those involving her peers. Young children are often just reluctant to engage in the situations, whereas older children usually describe the fear of being viewed negatively by others, or of embarrassing themselves. Your child might not speak to other children in school, avoid social gatherings such as parties, and try to hide when guests come to your house. Other things that socially anxious children commonly fear or avoid include eating in front of others, using a public restroom, speaking on the phone, addressing an unfamiliar adult such as a store clerk or waiter, and asking or answering questions in class. In severe cases, social anxiety can lead to a high level of self-isolation, with almost no contact with others. If your child is socially anxious, she may have difficulty making eye contact when interacting with other people, speak in a very soft tone of voice, or seem very rigid in her body language.

Selective mutism, which is commonly associated with social anxiety, is the term used to describe children who will completely avoid speaking in certain settings, despite being physically and mentally able to talk in other situations.

Generalized Anxiety

Generalized anxiety is more common in adolescents than in young, preadolescent, children, although many preadolescents have symptoms of generalized anxiety. Children with generalized anxiety have persistent worries about a variety of things and find it hard to control the worries. If your child has generalized anxiety, he may be preoccupied with things such as his school performance, his health or that of others, his social status, the family's income or stability, current events such as wars or epidemics, or his future success in various areas. He may be highly perfectionist and worry about small things and minor mistakes and errors, and he may have an overly critical view of himself and his performance. Such children may try to avoid activities if they are not certain that they will perform perfectly.

Children with generalized anxiety often have physical symptoms such as aches, pains, and upset stomach, and their mood may be grumpy or irritable. Concentration can also be negatively impacted in children with generalized anxiety. If your child has generalized anxiety, he may ask you many questions relating to his worries, seek a lot of reassurance, and prefer that you make decisions for him.

Phobias

Phobias are common in both children and adolescents and are among the most common mental health problems of childhood overall. Children with phobias have a strong and exaggerated fear of particular things or situations, and they can be fearful even at the prospect of an encounter with the thing they fear. Anything can be the focus of a child's phobia, but common phobias include animals and insects, heights, bad weather, water, darkness, small spaces such as elevators, airplanes, needles and blood, doctors and dentists, throwing up, clowns and costumed characters, loud noises, and choking. *food*

If your child has a phobia, she may try very hard to avoid any contact with the thing she fears. If she comes into contact with her phobia, or believes that she will, she may seem to panic and develop a racing heart, trembling, or vomiting. She also may become angry about having to confront her fear. Children with phobias often avoid even indirect contact with the object of their phobia, such as refusing to watch a movie with dogs in it because of a dog phobia, or avoiding any mention of the word dog. Your child may rely on you to help her avoid her phobia. She may ask you to promise that she will not have to face it, or have you check that the phobic thing is not present.

Panic and Panic Disorder

Panic attacks are considerably more common in adolescents than in younger children. Panic attacks are brief episodes of intense fear and physical arousal, usually lasting under 20 minutes. Any anxiety problem can trigger panic attacks, such as when a child with social anxiety has a panic attack before a performance. But panic attacks can also happen unexpectedly, without a clear reason or trigger. If your child has panic attacks, he may feel his heart racing and experience trembling, sweating, shortness of breath, chest discomfort or difficulty breathing, nausea, hot or cold chills, or numbness in parts of his body. During a panic attack children may have very frightening thoughts such as that they are dying or losing control over their minds, and they may experience a sense of unreality or detachment from themselves.

Panic Disorder occurs when children who have panic attacks become intensely worried about having additional attacks and adopt behaviors they believe will help them to avoid additional attacks. They may stop exercising because of the fear of triggering an attack, or they may avoid unfamiliar situations. If your child has panic disorder, he may ask you to accompany him places or to bring along special things such as extra water or a paper bag to breathe into.

Agoraphobia

Agoraphobia is also more common in adolescents than in young children and occurs when the fear of having panic-like symptoms causes a child to be fearful or anxious about various situations. Children with agoraphobia worry about experiencing panic symptoms and not being able to easily escape the situation or get help. They also may worry that having the panic symptoms in front of others, such as peers and classmates, will be embarrassing or humiliating.

Children with agoraphobia may try to avoid going to school, riding buses, going to movies or shows, or being in very open or very small and enclosed places. They may avoid crowds, and they may try to avoid leaving the house alone altogether.

Obsessions and Compulsions

Children with *obsessive-compulsive disorder* (OCD) have frequent obsessions and/or compulsions. *Obsessions* are thoughts, urges, or ideas that keep coming into the child's mind, causing discomfort or anxiety, and the child is unable to resist or control them. *Compulsions* are ritualized behaviors that the child repeats again and again, usually in an effort to ward off the obsessive thoughts or to prevent some negative event from happening. Although most children with OCD have a combination of both obsessions and compulsions, it is possible to have just one or the other. Children with OCD know that the thoughts are coming from their own minds. They also usually acknowledge that their compulsions do not actually serve a useful purpose in reality, although they feel unable to stop performing them. OCD occurs approximately equally in boys and girls, but tends to appear earlier in boys, with higher rates of OCD in preadolescent boys than girls.

Children with OCD may experience obsessive thoughts about things such as contamination and cleanliness, doubts about having done things, aggressive behaviors that they fear they will do or will be done to them or to others, negative events such as death and injuries, religion and god or the devil, hoarding and losing things, or sexual thoughts of various kinds. Sexual thoughts are more common in adolescents than younger children but can appear in younger, prepubertal, children as well. Your child may do various compulsive rituals such as washing and cleaning, arranging things a certain way, or checking repeatedly whether she has done something, such as turning off a light or packing her lunch. She may confess thoughts or actions unnecessarily, touch or tap things, walk or move in a special way, count things repeatedly, or avoid specific numbers. She also may attempt to create a sense of symmetry in her body, for example, by turning her head to the left if she turned it to the right, to "balance out" her body. Such children may seem overly scrupulous and rigid about right and wrong. They also may have fears of contamination not from germs or chemicals, but from other people. They may, for example, avoid looking at images of criminals because of a fear of becoming a criminal themselves.

In many cases there appears to be a logical, albeit unrealistic, connection between the obsessions and the compulsions. For example, a child with an obsession about losing things might repeatedly count the Legos in her toy box. In other cases, however, there does not appear to be a logical connection between the obsessions and the compulsions, as when a child counts her Legos because of an obsession about her parent having a car accident. Not performing the compulsion will almost always cause the child increased anxiety, and she may feel unable to refrain from the compulsive behavior for more than a short amount of time.

If your child has OCD, she may ask you for help in completing rituals. For example, she may ask you to listen to her confessions, wash her clothes more frequently, physically carry her in some places, or kiss her right cheek if you kissed the left one. Such children also may try to make you complete certain rituals yourself, such as washing your own hands excessively or repeating a special phrase.

Illness Anxiety

Children with *illness anxiety* are preoccupied with the possibility of becoming seriously ill. Their preoccupation is either completely unfounded or is highly exaggerated, relative to the actual risk. If your child has illness anxiety, he may become easily alarmed about his health, and he may try to confirm his health repeatedly through various checks or doctor appointments. On the other hand, a child with illness anxiety may try to avoid visiting doctors or hospitals because of the fear of discovering an illness or because of fear of infection. If your child has illness anxiety, he may ask you many questions about his health and about various illnesses, or try to engage you in research about diseases.

Avoidant/Restrictive Food Intake

Avoidant/restrictive food intake is not an anxiety disorder per se, but it is commonly associated with fear and anxiety. Children with avoidant/restrictive food intake may avoid foods based on sensory characteristics, for example, eating only dry foods, or only soft ones, or only foods of specific colors or shapes. Or they may avoid foods that they think can cause them harm, for example, eating only pureed food because of a fear of choking. Children with avoidant/ restrictive food intake are not attempting to lose weight, but their restriction can lead to low weight, slow growth, or reduced energy.

If your child has avoidant/restrictive food intake disorder, she may have difficulty in social settings, for example, avoiding playdates because of not being able to eat there. The problem can also impact family life, for example, by making it harder for a family to eat out, or requiring special food preparation at home.

Can Anxiety Be Treated?

Of all the emotional and mental health problems that occur during childhood and adolescence, anxiety is the most treatable. As explained in Chapter 1, normal healthy life is not free of anxiety and treating an anxiety problem does not mean that your child will never be anxious again. Your child may even still have a higher tendency to anxiety than many other children. The susceptibility to anxiety that caused your child to have a problem in the first place is probably not going to go away. But that does not mean your child has to have a significant anxiety problem forever. Successfully treating an anxiety problem means that children's day-to-day functioning is no longer significantly hampered by anxiety, and that they are free to live happier and more fulfilling lives.

Home, school, social interactions and relationships, as well as a child's personal sense of well-being can all be disrupted by an anxiety problem, and when a child overcomes his anxiety problem, all of these various areas of life can improve. For example,

- Home life can improve by having fewer arguments, and by the ability to make family plans that don't center on your child's anxiety.
- School life can improve as your child has an easier time going to school, paying attention and participating in class, and achieving to his academic potential.

- Social interactions and relationships can improve when your child is more interested in spending time with other people and becomes less inhibited when taking part in social activities.
- A child's personal sense of well-being can improve through experiencing less anxiety, better mood, and healthier living habits, such as better sleep and more healthful eating.
- A child's overall physical health can improve as a result of reduced anxiety.

Clinical trials, the scientific studies that test the effectiveness of various treatments, have repeatedly shown that treating anxiety works. Most children who receive treatment through clinical trials for anxiety no longer have a significant problem at the end of the treatment. And an even higher number indicate at least some degree of meaningful and significant improvement. Even a child who is not cured by treatment, and who still has an anxiety problem, will benefit from having that problem become meaningfully smaller.

It is quite common for a child who has overcome an anxiety problem to have to contend with high levels of anxiety again at some point in the future. Even after your child's anxiety has been successfully dealt with, the anxiety can come back. Although this can be discouraging, you and your child will have the knowledge that anxiety can be successfully reduced, and coping with it again will probably seem less daunting than it did the first time.

Research on childhood anxiety problems also shows that simply waiting for an anxiety problem to go away on its own does not usually work. In fact, children who have an anxiety problem and do not get help often get worse. For one thing, children with anxiety often avoid doing things that make them anxious. If this is the case for your child, she is missing out on opportunities to learn that she is able to tolerate and cope with anxiety, making her more likely to remain anxious.

When you put both things together, that is, the high likelihood of successfully addressing and reducing anxiety through effective treatment, and the low probability of child anxiety going away on its own, you end up with a very good reason to address the anxiety as soon as possible! Of course, all children will be anxious some of the time, and some fears are normal and to be expected during development. For instance,

- A child who exhibits social anxiety during the first week at a new school, may seem much less anxious in another week or two.
- A young child who expresses a fear of the dark may be showing a normal and natural tendency in children.

But most parents who are concerned because their child is anxious will have observed a much longer and more consistent tendency toward elevated anxiety in their child. If you have been aware of your child's anxiety for a significant amount of time, say more than a month or two, then taking steps to help the child become less anxious is probably wise. Furthermore, many of the steps and tools in this book can be useful even for children who only have occasional anxiety, or whose anxiety is not all that severe. Reading and working through this book will not require you to take your child to a doctor, or to enroll him in any form of specialized treatment. Learning these tools can help you respond to your child's anxiety in supportive and productive ways. You may benefit simply from having a plan and an understanding of how to help your child when he is anxious. And having these tools and this understanding may make it less likely that occasional or mild anxiety will grow into a more severe anxiety problem.

How Is Anxiety Treated by Professionals?

Treatments for childhood and adolescent anxiety have been studied through rigorous clinical trials and have been shown to work. In this section you will learn about these methods, and how you can use them to help your child. What all of these methods have in common, however, and what makes them different from the method described in this book, is that they all require your child's participation to be effective. In contrast, the method described throughout this book, which has also been studied through clinical trial research and found to be just as effective, *does not require your child to do anything at all.* Every step described later in this book requires only that you, the parent, complete it.

Why does this matter? Having a means of reducing your child's anxiety, without any need for her active engagement in the process, means that you can help your child whether she wants you to or not! I encourage you to read the rest of this chapter and to try to make use of the tools it describes, alongside the ones you will learn in the rest of this book. But if you find that your child is unwilling to work with you, you can focus on the tools that don't require her agreement. You may find that as her anxiety goes down, your child will become more willing to make use of the other tools, but if she remains un-willing, this illustrates why being able to treat your child's anxiety through your own set of tools is so useful.

Cognitive Behavioral Therapy

Cognitive behavioral therapy (CBT) is the most studied psycholog-ical treatment for childhood anxiety. Numerous clinical trials have shown it can be very effective in reducing anxiety in many children. CBT for anxiety focuses on several goals that correspond to the domains (areas) of child functioning that are impacted by anxiety:

Challenging Anxious Thoughts

The first step on the way to changing anxious thoughts is to become aware of them. Your child may be so used to thinking his anxious thoughts that he doesn't even realize that "it's anxiety talking." When you have identified the anxious thoughts that make your child feel scared, nervous, or worried, try challenging the thoughts by asking some questions about them. For example, you could ask, *how likely* is that thing to actually happen? Or *how bad would it be* if it actually happened? You may be surprised to realize that your child's answers are much more extreme than you would have expected.

Once you've identified your child's anxious thoughts, and helped him to challenge them by asking questions, it's time to come up with some alternative thoughts that are more realistic. Write down the alternative thoughts alongside the anxious ones together with your child, and try to keep practicing as much as possible. Don't expect that practicing these steps once or twice will have a large impact on your child's anxiety. Remember that he has been practicing the anxious thoughts for a long time!

Practicing Exposure

Exposure to feared objects and situations is considered by many professionals to be the most active ingredient in CBT for anxiety. Exposure is key to reducing avoidance and fostering more coping behavior. But exposures require that your child agree to participate, and it is not a good idea to force exposure on a child against her will. Practicing exposures often starts with creating a *fear hierarchy*, which is a list of different situations, ranked from easiest to hardest. Once you've created an exposure hierarchy, your child can start practicing working through the various steps. Encourage her to repeat each step on her hierarchy multiple times before going on to the next step.

Practicing Relaxation

Helping your child learn to take control of his body and cause it to relax can be a very powerful tool for reducing anxiety. The two systems most commonly targeted in learning relaxation are breathing and the muscles. Taking slow deep breaths for even one or two minutes can significantly lower anxiety. A good pace for the breaths would be about five seconds of breathing in and five seconds of breathing out. The whole cycle just takes ten seconds, meaning that practicing even ten slow breaths is already close to two minutes and would be a big step toward reducing your child's anxiety in that moment. Practicing muscle relaxation is another bodily skill commonly taught in CBT for anxiety. You can teach your child to focus on just one group of muscles at a time, holding them very taut and tight for about five seconds, and then letting go and allowing the muscles to relax. For most children, starting by tightening up the muscles is easier than trying to simply relax the muscles directly.

As with all the tools of CBT, you can only teach and practice relaxation if your child is willing to do it. It's not very relaxing to have someone force you to practice relaxation! So, if your child is not willing, let it go for now and try again another time.

Taking Control of Feelings

If your child is able to make herself feel a powerful feeling that is not fear, then she will probably feel less scared. One way to do this is through humor. If your child is able to make herself laugh, she will almost surely feel less afraid. Or, if laughing is too hard when your child is feeling scared, perhaps she can make herself feel angry instead. You could teach your child to become angry at her anxiety for tormenting her with annoying thoughts and lying to her about all the bad things that could happen. Once she starts getting mad, she is probably going to feel less afraid.

Additional Cognitive Behavioral Therapy Resources

There are several excellent books for parents that you can use to teach your child the skills of CBT and then practice them together. Appendix B at the end of this book is a short list of recommended books and resources that can help you to learn more about these tools, or to find a professional in your area with skill in delivering CBT.

Medication for Anxiety

Alongside CBT, the most studied treatment for anxiety in children is the use of medication. As with CBT, clinical trials have shown that many children who receive medication for anxiety get better. Some evidence suggests that the combination of psychological treatment and medication works better than either one alone, especially in severe cases of anxiety. Most professionals agree that a good strategy for most children is to start with psychological treatment and then introduce medication if the treatment is not working, or if the child is too anxious to participate. Most professionals also agree that even if a child is finding medication helpful, it is a good idea for the child to have psychological treatment also, so that he or she can learn more tools and skills for coping with anxiety.

Any decision to start, stop, or change a medication should always be done in consultation with a knowledgeable prescriber who has personally evaluated the child. Various kinds of medications are used for treating anxiety, and each has many specific names and brands. Many parents find these different options confusing, and the way psychiatric medications are classified adds to the confusion. For example, you might assume that the group of medications known as "anti-anxiety medication" would be the best choice for an anxious child. But, in fact, these medications are rarely a good choice, and it is far more common to prescribe an "antidepressant" when treating anxiety. If your child's doctor has prescribed an antidepressant, it is not because this prescriber is confused about your child's problem, but because these medications were used to treat depression before it became common to use them to treat anxiety. Even within the group of antidepressants, there are multiple kinds of medications. Consulting with an expert on the pharmacological treatment of anxiety is important before making any decisions about medication.

Most of the time medications for anxiety do not cause serious side effects and are tolerated well by children. However, if your child is taking a medication and complains of side effects, or if you notice something concerning, immediately contact your prescriber and explain what your child is experiencing. The prescriber will know whether a change in the dose or the medication is required.

Healthy Habits

Finally, before moving on to the method of reducing child anxiety that is the focus of this book, and that centers entirely around changes you make to *your* behavior, it is worthwhile considering whether your child's daily habits and routines are helping her . . . or helping her anxiety. Healthy eating, quality sleep, and physical activity can help to lower anxiety, whereas unhealthy habits can lead to higher levels of anxiety.

Does your child eat regular and nourishing meals? Does she consume a lot of caffeine? Caffeine is a stimulant in coffee, tea, cola drinks, and chocolate and can cause your child to be less relaxed and more antsy, jittery, or anxious. It also can prevent her from falling asleep easily and getting rest. Try to limit or completely eliminate caffeine intake for your child. Choose caffeine-free drinks and limit chocolate, especially around bedtime.

If your child is staying up very late at night, this is probably not helping with his anxiety either. Of course, it could be the anxiety that is keeping the child up at night, but as much as possible try to help him get a good night's sleep. Napping during the day can be very disruptive to nighttime sleep, so if your child is up at night try to prevent daytime napping.

Finally, encourage your child to be physically active during the day! A brief workout of any kind can be very useful in reducing anxiety, in addition to having other positive health benefits. Your child should get some form of exercise a few times a week. You can offer to go for brisk walks or runs together, or consider enrolling your child in a sport he enjoys.

In This Chapter You Learned:

- The main types of childhood and adolescent anxiety
- Whether anxiety can be treated
- How anxiety is treated by professionals

3

Is Your Child's Anxiety Taking Over Your Family?

Do Parents "Cause" Anxiety Problems in Their Child?

Childhood anxiety is not only a child problem—it is a child and parent problem. By saying this, I *do not mean that parents are the cause of anxiety in their children*. Parents of children with emotional or behavioral problems often find themselves accused of causing the problem in the first place. Sometimes this is said explicitly and directly, while other times it is insinuated or implied. You may have heard it in questions from teachers or therapists, and you may have seen it in looks from other parents. You may even have read scientific articles and research papers reporting on studies linking some parental characteristic to a childhood disorder. And yet, whether explicit or implied, this accusation is nearly always wrong. The idea that you, the parent, are the cause your child's emotional and behavioral problems stems in large part from (1) inaccurate assumptions about human development, (2) outdated psychological theories, (3) misunderstandings of research on the links between parental behavior and childhood disorders, and (4) an incorrect interpretation of family dynamics:

1. The assumption in human development that children are born "blank slates" and that their traits, both desirable and

43

problematic, come from their experiences during the so-called formative years of life, overlooks the large differences already present in infants from birth. Babies are not all the same. They have different temperaments and traits, challenges and strengths, and tendencies and predispositions. These innate differences, influenced by the genetic makeup of each individual child, are the building blocks of later personality. Yet if one believes in the "blank slate," then it is also natural to assume that parenting, which provides so much of the experience during those early years, is to blame for any problems a child might have.

2. The idea that parents are responsible for childhood problems (and even for problems that show up later in life) is at the heart of some of the most influential psychological theories of the past century. Psychiatrists, psychologists, and other mental health professionals have shaped people's understanding of themselves and their lives. The field of mental health has essentially taught the public that parents (especially mothers) are the root cause of all mental health concerns. Eating disorders, schizophrenia, autism—to name just a few—have been attributed to problematic parenting, in spite of no real evidence to back up these claims and considerable evidence to the contrary. It is no wonder that so many people assume that anxiety disorders as well must be caused by parents.

3. It is true that there is research supporting links between parental features and childhood problems. In the area of childhood anxiety disorders, much of this research has focused on parental behaviors (such as overprotection and criticism) and on the parents' own anxiety levels. Children who have high levels of anxiety tend to have parents who describe themselves as anxious or who have been diagnosed with an anxiety disorder. And parents who have a history of anxiety disorders are more likely than other parents to have at least one child who experiences anxiety symptoms. *Does this mean that parental*

anxiety causes childhood anxiety? NO! It means that there is a statistical link between the two things. Assuming that because two things are statistically linked, one has caused the other is a common mistake. There are, however, many reasons why two things may both happen without one being the cause of the other. Often there is a third factor, something that is not necessarily known, which may be the cause of both things. For example, parents and children may have similar levels of anxiety because of a genetic factor, or an environmental factor, such as poverty, could lead to both parent and child anxiety.

4. There is one final consideration that further rules out any reasonable basis for blaming parents for their child's anxiety problem. In most cases, parents who have a highly anxious child also have other nonanxious children. If parenting is a main factor leading children to develop anxiety problems, it seems likely that those other children also would have an anxiety problem. Of course, parents do behave differently with different children, and it may be that they are more protective or critical with one child than another, but we would still expect a much higher level of similarity in anxiety levels among siblings if parenting were the reason that children develop anxiety. Indeed, when parents do behave differently with one child than another, it is often because of differences in the child, who brings out different aspects in the parent. It is just as plausible for a child to shape parental behavior as for a parent to shape the child's anxiety.

How Does Your Child's Anxiety Impact You and Your Family?

Having, I hope, done away with the idea that parents are the cause of childhood anxiety problems, what does it mean to say that childhood anxiety is a child and parent problem? Very simply, this means that your child's anxiety problem is likely to have an impact on you, as the parent, and on the rest of the family. Of course, many other characteristics of your child also can impact you and your family to some extent. For example,

- If a child is continually expelled from school, the parents might end up missing work because of having to pick up or stay home with the child.
- A child with a physical illness may require special medical equipment that can be costly, or she may require adjustments to family life.
- If your child loves baseball, you may sign him up for a team, buy equipment, and the whole family might plan weekends to allow everyone to attend games.

Of course, this is true for childhood anxiety as well, but anxiety is "extra-special" when it comes to how it impacts parents and families.

If your child is highly anxious, this is likely to have a profound and extensive impact on you and your family. You may find that your child's anxiety seems to take over your lives, causing you to do things you would not normally do, or to stop doing things that you typically would do. You may realize that your time, whether at leisure or at work, is consumed by your child's anxiety. Your personal space may be greatly reduced, to the point where it seems that you don't have space of your own. And you may even feel as though your child's anxiety levels are "contagious," causing you to feel more anxious. You might even feel like a "sponge" soaking up all the anxiety from your child.

The reason that childhood anxiety, more than other problems, can have such a large impact on you as a parent is that when your child is feeling anxious, she probably looks to you to help her feel better. For example,

- If your child is worried, she might expect you to reassure her that things will be OK. This is completely natural and to be expected. But it means that you may find yourself rapidly becoming a "reassurer in chief," always expected to have the answers to make your child feel better, and always available to provide reassurance.
- If your child is scared of being alone, he might want to be near you, where he feels safer and more secure. This is also natural, but can quickly turn into you having to be near your child much of the time because he feels scared or is worried that he will feel scared if you're not nearby.
- If your child struggles with social anxiety and has a hard time speaking for herself, she may come to rely on you to help her navigate social situations, or to talk instead of her, and you may feel like you have turned into a mouthpiece, responsible for relaying your child's thoughts or wishes to the world.
- If your child is overly worried about his grades and gets upset at even small errors in homework, you may find yourself checking his homework for him multiple times, so that it starts to feel as if it is really your homework rather than his.

You may also realize that there are things you have stopped doing because you know that doing them could cause your child to become anxious or afraid. For example,

- If your child tends to become overanxious about current events and bad things in the news, you may have stopped reading the newspaper when she is around, or you may make sure not to have the news on TV when your child is home.
- If you know that your child has an excessive fear of insects, you may stop planning outings and picnics where he might have a scary encounter with a caterpillar or a bee.

- Perhaps you have stopped having friends over because you know that your child becomes upset at encounters with people outside the immediate family.
- Many parents with anxious children also realize that they have given up things such as going out in the evening, because it does not feel worth the anxiety it causes in their child.

These are just a few examples of the many different ways that anxiety in a child can impact you as a parent and affect the family overall. Later in this book you will learn to identify these changes for yourself, and you will learn how important a tool changing these behaviors can be for helping your child to become less anxious. But why are anxious children so reliant on parents? Why do almost all parents of anxious children describe having made at least some changes to their lives? The reason has to do with the very nature of anxiety in our species.

Why Do Children Rely on Parents When They Are Anxious [Hint: It's in Our Nature]

Most parents of highly anxious children describe their children's anxiety as having some impact on the parents' own lives, and many feel as though the child's anxiety has taken over the parent's life completely. By their very nature, children tend to involve their parents in their anxiety symptoms. And as the parent of an anxious child, you are also naturally inclined to step in and become involved in the anxiety symptoms. The reason for this pattern, seen almost universally in families with anxious children, has to do with the way anxiety works in mammals, including human beings.

Like many other species, both mammalian and not, human children are born defenseless. A baby left entirely alone would not survive, and the reason that children do survive, of course, is that they are *not* left to fend for themselves. They have parents and other caregivers who provide for them and protect them until they mature enough to take over the responsibilities of keeping themselves alive. When a baby or young child feels threatened or afraid, his natural response is to enlist the help of a caregiver. In other words, the natural response to fear in a young human being is a *social response* that involves signaling their caregivers so that the caregiver can act on the baby's behalf. Likewise, babies are not very skilled at calming themselves once the danger has passed, and they will stop crying only when their caregiver calms them by holding, rocking, or another soothing behavior. This natural tendency of your child to look to you for protection and reassurance when feeling worried, scared, or stressed is essentially hardwired into his brain. We all come from a long line of babies who made it to adulthood by relying on caregivers for protection and regulation, and we have inherited the natural tendency to rely on caregivers for these things during childhood.

Most of us were also children whose parents were aware and sensitive enough to notice if we were in danger and then act to protect us, and this tendency is also hardwired into our brains as parents. When our child is feeling anxious, it is in our nature to notice, and to be motivated to help her by providing protection until the threat has passed, and then to soothe her until she is calm again. Ignoring a child who is feeling anxious goes against our natural instinct and inclination, just as it goes against a child's instinct to feel anxious and not let her parents know.

What does all this mean for childhood anxiety problems? If your child is experiencing high levels of anxiety, even if she is not in any kind of danger and even if her anxiety is misplaced, it is likely that she is going to signal that anxiety to you, the parent. It is also likely that as the parent, you are going to take action to help your child be safe and calm. Even when you know that your child's anxiety is not realistically justified, and that she is actually quite safe, you are still going to feel motivated to help her *feel* safe. Recall the discussion earlier about our uniquely human ability to respond to imaginary threats much the same as we respond to real ones. It is entirely possible for us to feel scared or anxious even when there is no actual danger. And when your child is frightened, whether because of a real or unreal threat, she is going to respond in the same way—by signaling to you, the parent, that she is in danger, and relying on you to make the feeling of threat go away.

As the parent of a child, especially a young child, you possess a kind of superpower, which is the power to help make your child feel safe and secure just by being with him and interacting with him in a calming manner. This is an amazing power and can fill a parent with a sense of satisfaction like no other. But when your child suffers from anxiety and comes to continually rely on your superpower to feel better, it can start to feel more like a burden than a gift. When this happens, it may be time to start changing the game a little, by focusing on the long term rather than on the short term. Instead of helping your child not to feel anxious *right now*, it becomes important to help him become less anxious overall. The process described in this book is a method for achieving that longer term goal. Sometimes that will mean giving up the short-term goal of helping your child to feel less anxious *in the moment*, and accepting that he will be anxious right now. But the result of engaging with this process can be a child who is less anxious overall, leading to a better existence for both your child and yourself.

In This Chapter You Learned:

- Whether parents cause anxiety problems in their children
- How your child's anxiety impacts you and your family
- Why children rely on their parents when they are anxious

4

Common Pitfalls in Parenting
an Anxious Child

Protecting and Demanding

Being the parent of a child means facing endless challenges and dilemmas, from the big picture questions of how to help a child with a problem, to the many little decisions we make each day and even the words we choose when speaking to the child. A child's anxiety can make all of these decisions more complicated and more difficult, and there is no obvious answer for how best to approach these challenges.

Parents of children with anxiety often describe pitfalls and traps that their child's anxiety creates, and in this chapter, I describe some of those traps and ways to avoid them. Importantly, I am not suggesting that choices or mistakes you may have made as a parent are the reason your child is anxious. This chapter covers some of the pitfalls that can occur when you have a child who *is* anxious, and regardless of what caused the anxiety problem, when your child is anxious, *how* you respond and the attitudes you hold can matter.

Many of these traps and pitfalls can be loosely categorized as either "protective" or "demanding," which are broad categories of beliefs and behaviors, and each can be expressed in many different ways. As you read this chapter, try to think about which of these thoughts or behaviors seem to describe you. When you notice that one of them sounds like you, write it down. And then try to come up with one or two examples from your life of how it applies to you. You can use Worksheet 2 (Parenting Traps) in Appendix A at the end of this book to take some notes, which you will refer back to later.

The first category is that of *protection*, which covers thoughts and behaviors that center around the goal of protecting your child from harm or distress. Of course, protection is important, and if you think your job as a parent involves protecting your child from harm, then I agree with you! If your child is in actual danger, then of course protecting them becomes an important, indeed, the most important, role you have as a parent. If, however, your child is not in danger, that protection is not necessary and is misplaced. Parents of anxious children often realize, upon reflection, that they have become protectors when protection is not really needed. Focusing on protection much of the time can get in the way of other important goals, and when that happens, the protection is not only unnecessary, it actually becomes an obstacle. As you will also see, taking on the role of protector for your child, when a danger is not present, can convey to your child that she is in need of protection, making her feel less safe and more vulnerable.

The second category is that of *demanding*. Demanding is when you expect your child not to feel anxious, or to be able to act as though he is not, despite the very real anxiety that he is feeling. Like protection, demanding has an important place in parenting. If we placed no demands on our children, how would they learn to behave, and how would they be able to accomplish things that require effort or perseverance? But like protection, demanding can be misplaced or ineffective. If you are demanding that your child not feel something that he does feel, this demand is not likely to actually change his feeling. And if you demand that he act as though he is not anxious, without acknowledging how hard that actually is, this demand is not likely to succeed. Simply because something is not anxiety provoking to you as a parent does not make it any less anxiety provoking to your child.

Demanding also has another important limitation that makes it almost entirely unhelpful when dealing with child anxiety. When we are demanding something, we are demanding it of someone else. When a demand we make is not met, we often respond with frustration or anger because we feel helpless to enforce the demand or undermined by the lack of compliance. This can lead to conflict and hostility. In the method described in this book, you will not be required to make *any* demands on your child. Of course, this only applies to the steps you take to help your child become less anxious. Demands that relate to other parts of their lives and functioning will continue. But in helping your child to become less anxious, there will be no need to demand anything of her. So following the steps outlined in this book should not lead to increased anger or frustration in you. Some suggestions may make your child upset with you when you implement them, but that is a temporary reaction and will pass. In the meantime, you will be able to remain calm and not become angry because you have not demanded anything your child has not done.

Are You a Protective Parent?

If your child is highly anxious, you may feel compelled to protect him from the harms he fears. For example, if your child views social events as threatening because of the risk of embarrassment or humiliation, you may act to shield him from social situations. Or if your child is very anxious about tests and worries that she won't do well enough, you may try to prepare her for the test or make sure she has extra time to take it so that she can get the best grade possible. Remember, if any of these examples resonate with you, use Worksheet 2 (Parenting Traps) to jot them down.

Another kind of protection is even more common. It happens when you try to protect your child from the anxiety itself and the bad feelings it causes. Wanting to protect your child from feelings of anxiety is the most natural thing in the world. After all, what parents wants their children to be anxious, or to suffer distress of any kind? It is probably very plain to you that the anxiety is highly uncomfortable for your child, and it is natural for you want to help her avoid that discomfort in any way you can. Both kinds of protection—from the harms your child fears and from anxiety and distress—are natural parental reactions to child anxiety. But they're also traps that can trip up both the parent and the child.

When you are protecting your child from the harms that she fears, your behavior seems well aligned with your child thoughts and beliefs. But therein lies the trap. If your child's fears are misplaced, and if you hope that she will one day realize this and stop fearing those things, then a response that aligns with those fears is also going to be misplaced. Remember how anxious children have difficulty assigning accurate probabilities to various events, and how they tend to assign high value to negative events, making such events seem more negative than they actually are? Well, consider what your child is learning through your protection. In the example of the child who is scared of social situations because of the possibility that such events will end in embarrassment, that anxious child is probably viewing a negative outcome as more likely than is realistic. And he is probably viewing the possibility of being embarrassed as a catastrophic disaster, rather than as a temporary unpleasantness. If you, as the parent, are acting to protect your child from these social situations, then doesn't this seem to suggest that you also see the negative outcome as likely? Otherwise, why prevent the possibility? And doesn't it also seem to confirm that being embarrassed in a social situation is a really terrible thing? Otherwise, why are you making sure that your child doesn't take that risk? It's similar for the child who is worried about not acing a test. If you as the parent spend a lot of extra time learning and relearning all the material with your child, doesn't that seem to show that you also think that a less than perfect grade is a disaster? You may really be thinking that the negative outcomes (being embarrassed, not acing the test) are actually not all that likely, or not such a big deal, but even if you say that to your child, your protective behaviors convey the opposite.

Imagine that your child was just diagnosed with a chronic condition, say asthma or diabetes. It's a new thing for the whole family and everyone is getting used to the idea that this problem is not going to go away anytime soon. What would you want your child to know about what it's going to be like? If you could tell him one thing that he would believe, what would it be? Perhaps that it's going to be OK, or yes, it's a challenge, but he can handle it and still have a great life despite the problem. You would never tell him the opposite! You definitely wouldn't sit your child down and say something like, "What a shame that it has to be you with the diabetes; you're really not a kid who can cope with this kind of thing." Of course you would never say anything like that! You'd want your child to know that he can handle it, that he's *strong enough, and that even if it's hard, it will be OK. Isn't that also what you'd want to say to a child with anxiety? That it's hard, but he is strong enough to have anxiety and still be OK!*

Trying to protect your child from anxiety and distress is also a reasonable thing to do, but this kind of protection can reinforce a child's anxious beliefs. Take another example, say a child who is worried about becoming ill with a serious disease. As the parent you can see how troubling this thought is to your child, even though you know that she is healthy and the likelihood of her developing a serious illness is very low. You might want to help your child stop those anxious and worried thoughts, so she can feel better and be less worried. Perhaps you reassure her repeatedly that she is not going to be sick, maybe going as far as to promise her that she will be fine. Or perhaps you spend time with her researching various illnesses in the hope that she will be convinced by the information and stop worrying. Or maybe you even take her to doctors to assure her that she is well. None of these behaviors is intended to protect your child from being sick; rather, they are intended to help the child not feel so worried and anxious. But this is also a trap. All these behaviors are showing your child that being anxious is a very negative thing, to be avoided even at great cost. The next time your child has a worried thought, she would then be likely to believe that it, too, must be done away with, and that she has no alternative but to seek more reassurance from you in a never ending cycle.

Anna was terrified of her house being broken into. She would lie in bed, and her brain would fill with pictures of a burglar in black clothing and a mask looming over her bed. She would see the burglar in the shadows of the things around her room and hear him in the creaks and sounds of the old house. Sometimes Anna would wake up in the middle of the night and lie there in her bed trembling with fear for a long time until she fell back asleep. One time she even had a nightmare of a burglar kidnapping her and when she woke up, she was sure it had been real.

Anna's father, Bryson, decided something had to be done. He went out and purchased a new lock—the best and biggest he could find—for the front door. He had the lock installed and showed it to Anna so she could see the home was protected. "See Anna," he said, "I'm not going to let anything happen to you!" That night Anna again woke up from a nightmare about burglars in the house. Her mother tried to comfort her, but Anna was sobbing and took a long time to calm down. She told her mother, "Even Daddy thinks burglars are coming. He got a big lock to keep them out!"

Do any of the following statements sound like you?

- *Anxiety is harmful and can cause children to be scarred or damaged.*
- *Your job as a parent is to make your child's life as comfortable as possible.*
- *You want to help your child feel good all the time.*
- *Your child is more vulnerable than other children.*
- *You want people to go easy on your child because of the anxiety.*
- *You try to remove obstacles and challenges from your child's path.*
- *Your child can't handle stress.*
- *Your child needs a softer touch.*

If some of these statements (or others like them) sound like you, then write them down on Worksheet 2 (Parenting Traps), along with one or two examples from your life.

The above statements are typical of parents who are protecting their child. Hidden inside them are underlying beliefs that can get in the way of helping your child to be less anxious. For example, the statements "anxiety is harmful" and "anxiety is damaging" are tricky. We know that exposure to extreme levels of anxiety, as in the case of very traumatic events, can indeed be harmful. Post-traumatic stress is a real thing that can be highly disruptive to life and can lead to long-term impairment. But post-traumatic stress does not occur because of normal events in your child's daily life. These normal events can cause anxiety, but that anxiety is actually *not* dangerous. If you believe that *any* anxiety is harmful, then it makes sense for you to try to help your child always avoid being anxious. But this, as you already know, is not possible. And because your child is going to feel anxious sometimes, she will benefit from believing that she is capable of coping with anxiety and that it does not always have to be avoided. Think about how bad it would feel to know there is a terrible thing that can cause you damage and suffering and there is no way to avoid it. Much better for your child to know that regular anxiety is not dangerous and is, in fact, something she can cope with when she has to.

Another belief, similar to the thought that anxiety is harmful and must be avoided, is reflected in the statement, "My job is to make my child's life as comfortable as possible." Of course most parents would prefer that their child be comfortable, but is that really the most important job of a parent? *Preparing your child for life in the world can also mean helping him to be strong enough to cope with the less comfortable aspects of life.* Do you expect your own life to always be easy? Do you expect to always feel comfortable yourself? Probably not. And if you do, you are probably frustrated much of the time by the reality of not always feeling at ease and comfortable. If you are able to cope with the challenges of your own life, it is probably because you are able to accept not being comfortable some of the time and to take things in stride. Anxious children also can learn to take things in stride, even their own anxiety. A wise quote I heard recently says it nicely: "We might consider our role as parents not to be to reduce the pain our children must live through, but to help them learn how to suffer less."

Teaching your child not to fear anxiety and to take it in stride is one of the biggest gifts you can give your anxious child. It is an unfortunate fact, but a child who is highly anxious today is likely to experience a higher than average level of anxiety throughout much of his life. This does not mean he needs to suffer from an anxiety disorder or be impaired by anxiety his whole life. It does mean, however, that anxiety is likely to be one persistent or recurring aspect of his life, which makes it all the more important to learn that he is quite capable of coping with anxiety.

The other statements listed above reflect similar beliefs, which sound plausible but are actually traps that can ensnare parents coping with child anxiety. Making it your job to "remove obstacles and challenges from your child's path" or to ensure that the world "goes easy on them" because they are "more vulnerable" or "can't handle stress" all have the potential to reflect to your child an image of herself as weak and unable to cope without you always being there to clear the way. These thoughts can turn you into a kind of mine-sweeper for the minefield of your child's life. You may want to clear as many hurdles as possible from her way, but she can be left with the sense that the world really is full of mines, and that she can't clear them on her own.

Another risk in trying to clear the mines from your child's path is an important one to consider. Because you can't control most of the world, your ability to protect your child is largely limited to the things that happen in your home. In your home, you can try to ensure that as few triggers for your child's anxiety are in place as possible, but the world outside your door is unlikely to be as con-siderate. As a result, your child may feel safe only at home, and many anxious children increasingly avoid contact with the world outside. As parents work to create a sheltered environment that does not provoke their child's anxiety, the world at large can seem more and more frightening. Real-life relationships can be replaced with virtual, online "friendships" that don't require coping with real human interaction; going to school can seem increasingly difficult and may be replaced with home schooling; even simply leaving the house can start to feel like a daunting task. In the most severe cases, the result is self-isolation and complete lack of functioning outside the home. Even if your child is not showing these signs, protective minesweeping increases the risk of isolation in the future.

Are You a Demanding Parent?

As noted earlier, the second category of parental traps that can ensnare parents of highly anxious children is that of *demanding* your child not feel anxious or that he behave as though he does not. Working through the steps in this book will create situations in which your child will be required to cope with his anxiety, but changing your behavior is very different from demanding that your child change his. As described in Chapter 2, treatment for anxiety often does focus on changing the child's behavior. But that kind of treatment relies on a child choosing to engage with the therapy and not on parents imposing the changes on the child. When parents expect their child to undertake these changes without the necessary motivation and willingness on the child's part—that is when the parents are being demanding.

> *Grant was six years old and scared of water. He would not go to the pool or to the beach, and when his family had a lakeside get-together with friends, he refused to get in any of the boats or wander close to the water. Instead he spent much of the afternoon in the car, refusing to get out, and his parents took turn staying there with him to keep an eye on him.*

One summer day his mother, Carmen, decided enough was enough, and it was time to get over this problem. After she picked Grant up from camp, she drove straight to the local pool. When Grant realized they weren't heading home and asked where they were going, Carmen said, "You'll see when we get there." When they parked near the pool and Grant realized where they were going, he became very upset. He resisted getting out of the car and after his mother managed to get him inside the pool enclosure, with a combination of firm instructions and promises of rewards, he refused to change into the swimsuit she had brought for him. After a few minutes of arguing, his mother said, "Fine! Just sit there then, and watch me!" She changed into her swimsuit and dived into the water. Carmen swam a couple of laps, got out, and walked back to Grant. "See, nothing happened!" she said. "Just look around you. Everyone here is swimming and playing in the water. Nobody is scared and everyone is having fun. You just need to get over this and do it already."

Grant didn't answer and avoided her gaze, staring resolutely at the ground. Carmen felt frustrated and started getting annoyed. "Grant! I'm speaking with you, look at me!" When the boy looked up, she continued. "Did you hear what I told you? You have to do this and stop being a baby about it. If you don't start swimming, you'll be scared of water forever. Do you want that? Here, you can start by getting in the kiddie pool. The water isn't even deep enough to reach your waist for god's sake. You can't feel scared of water that doesn't reach your waist! What do you think will happen? You're going to drown in knee deep water with me standing right next to you?!"

Grant was crying now and still wouldn't budge. Carmen realized that other parents had begun to observe her interaction with her son, and feeling too uncomfortable to continue, she picked Grant up and left the pool in frustration.

Carmen's frustration and exasperation with her son are understandable. His fear is clearly exaggerated, and it is interfering not only with his own activities, but with the entire family. It has even disrupted social gatherings, as when his parents had to sit with him in the car while visiting with friends. Carmen probably also understands that Grant's avoidance is maintaining his fear of the water, and as long as he continues to avoid any contact with water, it is unlikely that he will overcome his fear. The mother believes that enough is enough and it's time for the child to get over this problem once and for all. But her effort to break through the wall and get Grant to overcome his fear ends in more frustration and disappointment for both of them. Grant is now even less likely to be willing to approach the water, and Carmen may not be eager to try again any time soon. Her desire to help Grant ended up causing her to act in a demanding way that ultimately had the opposite effect.

Do any of the following statements sound like you?

- *She just needs to get a grip.*
- *He's just looking for attention.*
- *The world is not a place for sissies.*
- *Stop being a baby!*
- *Just look at me; see I'm not afraid!*
- *Suck it up!*
- *Just do it already.*
- *Why are you making a big deal out of this?*
- *We can't let fear control us.*
- *Nobody else acts this way.*
- *Why can't she be more like her sister?*

If some of these statements (or others like them) sound like you, then write them on Worksheet 2, along with one or two examples from your life.

Demanding that Your Child *Feel* Differently

When Carmen said to Grant, "You can't feel scared of water that doesn't reach your knees," she may not have meant the statement literally. It is, of course, possible to be frightened of knee-high water, just as it is possible to be frightened of anything else—even things that don't exist. It is likely that what Carmen really meant is something like, "It makes no sense to be scared of knee-high water," or, "There's no need to be scared of it," or perhaps, "Gosh, I wish you would stop being scared of the water." But what Carmen actually said to her son is that she doesn't believe it's possible for him to feel what he feels. Have you ever had someone tell you that you feel differently than you actually feel? It's not a pleasant experience and almost nobody appreciates it! In fact, when someone tries to tell us what we feel, the experience is intrusive and we usually dig in, defending the integrity of our own feelings. Telling Grant that he doesn't feel scared, even if that's not precisely what Carmen meant, is likely to make him more resolute and less open.

Even if Grant knows that his mom means he *shouldn't* feel scared, and believes that he actually does, the experience is still unpleasant. Grant can't simply choose to feel differently, so telling him that he should feel otherwise is essentially telling him that his feelings are not OK. Words like "should" don't really apply to things like feelings and thoughts. It's meaningless to say that someone should feel a certain way when they don't. All this can accomplish is to cause that person to feel either guilty or ashamed for not feeling as they should, or rejected for how they do feel.

Demanding that a child feel differently can happen in both subtle and extreme ways. An example of a subtle demand is when a child says, "It's scary," and a parent responds with, "No it's not." That parent is not trying to tell the child to feel differently, but by insisting that something is not scary, the parent is telling the child that how she feels is wrong. A more accurate, and less demanding, statement would be, "It's not scary *for me*," or perhaps, "It's not dangerous." Things can be safe and still scary, so saying something is not dangerous is not the same as demanding a child feel differently, it is simply providing more objective information. And saying, "It's not scary for *me*," acknowledges that the parent and the child are different people, who can have different feelings.

More extreme forms of demanding that a child feel differently can arise when a parent becomes angry or frustrated, or believes that she can motivate a child by making him feel badly or embarrassed about the fear. In the earlier example, notice how as Carmen became increasingly upset with Grant, the things she said to him became increasingly harsh and judgmental. First, she tells him to look around at all the other children who are not afraid, something he already knows and is likely ashamed about. Then she tells him to "stop being a baby," and finally, as her patience runs out, she ridicules his fear by asking if he really thinks he is going to "drown in knee-high water." Carmen is not trying to be mean or hostile to Grant. She is simply feeling unable to help him overcome his fear and disappointed that her latest attempt has failed because of what seems like his unwillingness to work with her.

Demanding that Your Child *Do* Differently

Another kind of demanding is when a parent makes a demand of their child to act as though the child is not scared, even though he is. When Carmen tells Grant, "You have to do this and stop being a baby about it," she is demanding that he overcome his fear right then and there and cope with something that for him is still terrifying. Grant is left with what seems like an impossible choice: He can get in the water even though he is very scared and feels unable to do so, or he can disobey his mother and make her angry and upset with him. It's no wonder that Grant tries to avoid the situation entirely by avoiding her gaze and staring at the floor without answering her. Faced with such a controlling demand from his mother, opting out of the interaction entirely is the only kind of control he has left.

But If Only She'd Try, She'd See It's OK

This may well be true! It is a very common thing to see a child who is scared of doing something new for the first time try it out after a lot of encouragement, only to immediately want to do it again (and again and again…). You may be feeling, as a parent, that if your child were to try just once, to just get over that fear one time, she would realize she is not scared anymore at all. This belief can really push you into overdrive! Believing that the solution to the problem is so close, if only you could get your child to face her fear just one time, can make you push very, very hard to get her to do it. But there is one thing you should know. The pattern of a child trying something once, realizing she isn't scared, and never having a problem with it again, is much more typical of normal fears than it is of chronic and persistent anxiety. A child who is afraid to ride the roller coaster and is talked into getting on it may well get off and run straight back to the line to get back on again. But a child with a severe and persistent fear of heights who is talked into getting on the roller coaster is much less likely to do so.

The important thing is not only whether your child will be happy with the result of the ride, it's also whether you can talk her into getting on in the first place. Children with an anxiety problem are unlikely to feel encouraged by the kind of demands that deny the validity of what they are feeling and are less likely to be swayed by such demands. Increasing the pressure you place on your child to ignore her fear is likely to get her to simply dig in and insist that she cannot do it. Anxious children are more likely to try something new if you acknowledge that they have a choice in the matter and accept that it is hard for them.

You're Superman—I'm Not!

Another way of demanding that your child feel differently is by trying to show him how he should be feeling. This happens, for example, when you as a parent say something such as, "Look at me. See, I'm not afraid," with the implication being, "and neither should you be." Carmen told Grant to stay in his seat and look at her while she swam a few laps and then returned to him saying, "See, nothing happened." The problem is that while your child may admire you for not being afraid, it doesn't mean that he is any less afraid! In fact, many anxious children do feel admiration for their parents who clearly don't share their fears. But as one child said to me, "My dad is superman—doesn't mean I can fly!" Knowing that the parent is superman doesn't bring the child any closer to being able to fly. The child may feel admiration, or he may feel small and weak in comparison, but either way, he is just as non-superman as ever. Showing your child that you *do* feel fear just like him, that you are not superman, and that you cope with the same kinds of challenges, is much likelier to help your child believe that he can cope, too. From the child's perspective:

> If my parent is not superman and has fears and stresses just like me but is able to overcome them, well, that might not be as cool as having superman in the family, but it does mean that I may be able to cope like my parent. And it also means my parent has a better chance of understanding me and what I am feeling.

In This Chapter You Learned About:

- Protecting and demanding in response to child anxiety
- Whether you are a protective parent
- Whether you are a demanding parent

5

Family Accommodation

Jill is 12 years old and constantly worries that one of her parents will become seriously sick. She asks each of her parents about their health many times a day. Last year Jill's dad jokingly offered to do 30 sit-ups in front of her just to "prove" how healthy his heart was and to show that he was in shape. Since that day, Jill has begged him to "do the sit-ups" every day and will cry if he refuses. Now Jill has started asking her mom to do sit-ups as well!

Malik is 10 years old and afraid to go to sleep in his bed alone. He says he sometimes hears noises and is worried that a burglar might be in the house. Malik would like his mother, Kiara, to sleep next to him, but she has a lot of housework to take care of. Kiara has tried putting a white-noise machine in Malik's room so that he won't hear noises at night. Now Malik is afraid that his mother might leave the house and he won't hear her. So every night Malik lies in bed, and his mother deliberately makes a lot of noise from the kitchen, banging pans and dishes, so that he hears her and knows she's there. Unfortunately, all the noise Kiara makes actually keeps Malik from falling asleep.

Fiona is nine years old and has been extremely anxious ever since she saw a film of the Twin Towers falling after the attacks of 9/11. She had nightmares for the first few nights and became worried about a tower falling on her or her family. Her parents thought it was a normal reaction at first and tried to reassure her. They realized the problem was more serious, however, when Fiona had a massive meltdown when they parked their car near a tall building one day. Fiona cried and seemed to be having a very uncharacteristic temper tantrum until they agreed to move the car farther away from the building. Since then, Fiona has resisted getting into the car unless her parents promise not to drive or park near a tower, which now describes any tall structure including buildings, smokestacks, and cell-phone towers. Fiona's family has mapped out towers in their area and her parents always make sure to avoid them when driving.

In previous chapters you saw how children are naturally hardwired to rely on parents for help when they are feeling anxious. In this chapter we will turn things around and talk about your child's anxiety from your perspective as a parent. After all, not only children want their parents to help them feel better. You are also powerfully motivated to help your child. As the parent of a child with an anxiety problem, you probably have made many changes to your own behavior. For example,

- You find yourself answering your child's questions repeatedly or providing constant reassurance.
- Your child's anxiety has led to changes in the family's sleeping arrangements and nighttime rituals.
- You avoid going places that you know will trigger your child's anxiety.
- You answer questions that are directed at your child because you know that speaking to other people makes her uncomfortable.

If you've made changes like these, rest assured—you're not alone!

When we asked hundreds of parents of anxious children if their children's anxiety had led to changes in their own behavior, 97% described making these kinds of changes. Providing repeated reassurance was the most frequent behavioral change reported by the parents. Many other studies from around the world show that parents from all walks of life, and even from different countries and cultures, report that having an anxious child leads to similar changes in their own behavior.

What Is Family Accommodation?

Family accommodation is the term used by psychologists to describe the changes that parents make in their own behavior to help their children avoid or lessen feelings of anxiety. Table 5.1 describes some common forms of family accommodation and how they relate to children's anxiety problems and symptoms.

Participation and Modification

Family accommodation can take a limitless variety of forms, but it can be useful to group these forms into two main categories: (1) Participation in anxiety-driven behavior and (2) Modification of family routines and schedules.

Participation in Anxiety-Driven Behavior

Participation in anxiety-driven behavior occurs when you are actively engaging in a behavior with the aim of avoiding or reducing your child's anxiety. Sleeping next to your child is an example of a participation accommodation. Answering the same question over and over is another example. These active-participation accommodations can take up a significant amount of time each day. They can also be costly. The mother of a child with obsessive-compulsive disorder (OCD) who was buying large quantities of toilet paper because her child could not shake the feeling that he wasn't quite clean enough calculated that she was spending close to $100 each month on toilet paper! She also had to pay a plumber to unclog the pipes twice in one year. In another example, a child who was afraid of becoming

TABLE 5.1. Common Forms of Family Accommodation

Child Anxiety Problem	Symptom	Family Accommodation
Social Anxiety	Child was uncomfortable when guests came over to visit	Parents stopped inviting guests over when the child was home
	Child looked away and did not answer when a waiter asked what she would like to order for dinner	Parents always ordered for their child and answered any questions from the waiter
Generalized Anxiety	Child was worried that mom would have a car accident	Mother would repeatedly pinky swear to drive carefully, and she would text the child when she arrived at work
	Child was worried that his homework was not perfect	Dad would check the homework each day and review it several times with the child
	Child was worried about becoming seriously sick	Parents would repeatedly explain to the child that she is healthy and would answer many questions about health and illness
Obsessions and Compulsions	Child was afraid of becoming contaminated by germs	Mom would only use new, previously unopened, food products, such as ketchup or yogurt, and would throw away any leftovers
	Child was compulsive about the number three	Parents would turn lights on or off three times if the child was in the room
	Child was afraid she had done something bad and would be punished	Mom or dad would listen to the child's "confessions" each day and promise the child she had not committed a sin or a crime

TABLE 5.1. Continued

Child Anxiety Problem	Symptom	Family Accommodation
Separation Anxiety	Child was afraid to stay alone at birthday parties, playdates, or sports events	Parents would stay with the child until it was time to leave
	Child was afraid to stay in bed alone at night	Mom or dad would lie near the child until he fell asleep, or bring the child to the parents' bed to sleep
	Child would have a meltdown if she could not see her mother	Mom would keep the door open while using the toilet
	Child was afraid to stay with a babysitter in the evening	Parents did not go out in the evening together
Phobia of Vomiting	Child was afraid to become carsick	Family did not take drives of more than 45 minutes
	Child was afraid of catching a sickness and vomiting	Parents kept child home from school if somebody in the class had been sick the day before
Phobia of Insects	Child was afraid to be outside in the spring or summer	Family avoided all picnics or field trips
	Child was afraid of insects in the home	Parents would search for insects with the child for 30 minutes every evening before bedtime
Phobia of Costumed Characters	Child is afraid of any mention of people in costumes	Parents refrain from mentioning costumes and avoid all discussion of them

sick avoided all leftovers, as well as any food that was within one week of its expiration date, leading parents to throw away food that was still good and to buy new food in its place.

The cost of accommodations in terms of time taken can be just as high. The father of a boy in high school described standing outside his son's classroom for several hours each morning because the child was afraid to go in unless his dad promised to stay. A mom who was answering her phone many times during each work day to reassure her child that she would be home on time, felt she was no longer able to function competently at her job because of the accommodation.

Modification of Family Routines and Schedules

Modification of family routines and schedules is when you make changes to the patterns of your daily life because of your child's anxiety. Examples include no longer inviting guests over to the home because social interactions make your child anxious, or returning home early from work, or going to work later than you otherwise would. Not taking vacations that would trigger anxiety, for example, when a child has a fear of water or flying, is another modification accommodation. Often these modification accommodations have gone on for so long that they seem normal. One mother regularly turned down promotions at work because she knew her child would be upset if she had to travel for her job.

Modification accommodation can impact the entire family, not just the parents. Siblings may be impacted as their own needs or plans shift to accommodate for their sibling's anxiety. Recognizing the impact that family accommodation has on siblings is important, and we will discuss this issue more thoroughly at the end of this chapter. In this chapter you'll also learn about how accommodations can actually be unhelpful over time, maintaining rather than reducing your child's anxiety.

Are You Accommodating?

Probably! But that's OK. As I noted earlier, almost all parents who have an anxious child will find that they are accommodating their child's anxiety. The important thing is for you to become aware of your accommodations, so that you can plan what changes to make and how to make them.

You can start by asking yourself some simple questions and writing down the answers on Worksheet 3 (You and Your Child's Anxiety) in Appendix A at the end of this book:

- *How much of your time is taken over by your child's anxiety?*
- *What are you doing differently for this child, compared to his/her siblings?*
- *What would you do differently if your child was not anxious or afraid?*

Questions such as these will help you become aware of the family accommodations that you have been providing. If you live with a partner, it is a good idea to talk about this together. You each may be able to point out accommodations that the other is not aware of. But don't be critical! This is not an opportunity to tell each other off or to point fingers. It is an opportunity to reflect on how your child's anxiety has impacted your lives, and on the efforts you each have been making to help your child not feel scared. It also can be helpful to talk this over with trusted friends and relatives. Again, the point here is to gain insight and knowledge, not to criticize.

Later in this book you will learn how to identify, map, and monitor the various forms of family accommodation. You will learn how to reduce some of that accommodation to help your child grow stronger and less anxious. For now, just take the time to reflect and notice. Don't change anything yet. Reducing accommodation is important, but it is best done in a planned and thoughtful manner.

Noticing how you accommodate in day-to-day life will help you to choose the best accommodations to focus on, and to make the best plans to change your behavior in a helpful and supportive manner.

You Thought You Were Helping—Isn't That Your Job?

Olivia, the mother of a 13-year-old girl:

> When my daughter was diagnosed with a serious food allergy, the doctors told me about all the changes we would have to make as a family. How certain foods were dangerous for her and that we should always plan for a safe and healthy environment that would avoid her "trigger foods." When she became anxious, I thought we should do the same thing. Make sure that we kept her "triggers" away, and arrange our lives to not provoke her anxiety. What's the difference?

Helping your child cope with difficulty is one of the most important aspects of being a parent. From that first time you held your infant for a shot, to insisting she go to bed at night, to making him go to school in the morning, parenting is often about making tough choices. Providing too much accommodation for children's anxiety can be like telling them they don't need the shot after all—it will help them feel better in the moment, but it will put them at greater risk in the long term.

Ask yourself this question: *What is **the most important thing** for a child who is vulnerable to anxiety to learn?* I believe the answer is that the child **can cope with anxiety** and know that it's OK to feel anxious some of the time. After all, if your child is likely to experience a lot of anxiety in life (and current research suggests that an overly anxious child is likely to experience higher levels of anxiety over the course of her life), then the last thing you would want her to think is that she can't handle it! We want our children to believe that they can cope and to learn skills for coping most effectively. Thinking about anxiety like this makes it clear that *an important job for parents of anxious children is to instill in their children the knowledge that they are capable of coping with anxiety.* Consider the following anecdote, told to me by the father of an eight-year-old boy:

> It all started about six months ago. We were on a family trip in New York City and were having lunch at a bistro restaurant downtown. Rickie needed to use the bathroom before we left. He went to use the bathroom and we ordered the check. By the time we had paid for lunch and were ready to go, Rickie hadn't come back. I went to check on him and called to him from outside the door. Rickie was still inside and sounded stressed. He had been trying to open the door and hadn't been able to work the handle. I opened the door and saw that he was crying. I told him it's OK, that we wouldn't have left without him and that he was in no danger, but he was still upset. We tried to talk to him and explain that he wasn't actually locked in or trapped and that, of course, we would get him out. We asked him if he felt up to continuing the trip and Rickie just shrugged. He seemed to have lost the fun of the trip so we decided to cut it short and go home early. Next time we were in a restaurant, Rickie asked me to go to the bathroom with him. It was a single, but he wanted me to come inside with him, and I didn't want him to feel scared so I came in. Since that time his fear has only grown. He is afraid to go to the bathrooms in school and wants someone to stand right outside if he does. Whenever we suggest going out to eat, he becomes stressed so we've cut back on that a lot. We need help because now Rickie is starting to say that he won't go into the bathroom alone at home. He says he can't deal with it alone and that he needs us; that he won't go without us even if he has an accident. We've been going in with him, but it's becoming ridiculous. He just seems to be getting more scared despite all of our help.

Rickie had an unpleasant experience (getting stuck in a restaurant bathroom) and was understandably upset, and his parents did their best to reassure him. Now Rickie has become focused on avoiding similar unpleasant experiences in the future. He recalls the event vividly and is determined not to feel that way again. Like most children, Rickie is relying on his parents to help ensure that this doesn't happen, but every time he goes into the bathroom with his mom or dad, his belief that he cannot cope alone is being strengthened. He is not being given the opportunity to learn that he *can* cope. It is as though his parents are saying to him, "You can't deal with stressful things; you need us to deal with them for you." And like most children, as well as adults, he is experiencing one of the great ironies of anxiety: *The more you try to avoid feeling anxious, the more anxiety you are going to feel.* To help Rickie, his parents will have to shift their focus away from helping him not be scared in the bathroom and instead focus on teaching him that *he can be fine even if he does get scared.* This is a lesson that cannot be taught just with words, but that they will deliver very powerfully when they remove the family accommodation.

Good Accommodation and Bad Accommodation

The word *accommodation* has different meanings depending on the context, and in many cases it describes something very positive. Children with special needs, for example, are provided accommodations in school to help them achieve their potential. A child who is a slow writer might be afforded extra time on written tests, and this would be an important and positive accommodation. Another usage of the word accommodating is to describe someone who is easy to get along with, the opposite of stubborn or selfish.

Why is accommodating anxiety different? Why am I describing accommodation as a problem or as something to be reduced? When it comes to anxiety, not all accommodation is negative or unhelpful. Some accommodations can be useful in helping children to overcome their anxiety. In some cases, accommodations can act as scaffolding, propping children up and helping them to grow stronger and more independent. In many other cases, however, accommodation is actually doing the opposite of what we intend and is making the anxiety worse. Like Rickie's parents in the example above, you may be frustrated because your child seems to be growing more rather than less anxious, despite your accommodations. Figuring out which accommodations are helpful and which are unhelpful is an important step, and the best way to figure this out is to ask yourself the following:

- Is this accommodation helping your child to gradually cope more?
- Or is it helping your child to avoid more and more?
- Is this a step forward or a step backward, relative to how your child has been coping recently?

Accommodation is helpful when it is a step along the road toward increased coping. For example, when a child has not been able to attend school because of an anxiety problem, having him go to school accompanied by a parent can be a helpful accommodation. It will be a gradual step forward and the accommodation can be removed as coping increases. Accommodation is unhelpful when it means helping the child to avoid more, and to cope less. If your child has been attending school on his own, albeit with some difficulty, then deciding one day to accompany him to school would likely be an unhelpful accommodation.

Put another way, accommodation is helpful when it teaches your child the valuable lesson *that she is able to cope with feeling anxious.*

TABLE 5.2. Examples of Helpful and Unhelpful Accommodations

Situation	Helpful Accommodation	Unhelpful Accommodation
Your child calls you on the phone at work each day	You agree to call your child once each day to check in	You answer whenever your child calls and talk until she feels secure
Your child is afraid of messing up at baseball and does not want to go to practice	You agree to speak to the coach and explain your child's fears to him	You encourage your child to stay home so he won't feel bad
Your child is afraid to be alone in the shower and wants you to wait in the bathroom while she showers	You agree to go into the bathroom with her, and then to leave her there for a little longer each day	You stay in the bathroom whenever she showers
Your child is afraid to sleep alone in bed and has been coming into your bed in the middle of every night	You return your child to bed and stay with him for a few minutes as he relaxes and falls asleep	You put the child to sleep in your own bed so he doesn't need to get up at night

Accommodation is unhelpful when it reinforces your child's belief that she cannot cope with anxiety and must avoid situations that are likely to trigger it.

Table 5.2 provides some examples of helpful and unhelpful accommodations in coping with an anxious child.

It's So Hard Not to Accommodate!

Very true! Accommodation is hard, but not accommodating can be even harder. There are many reasons that not accommodating your child can seem like the harder choice. Let's look at some of the things that can make removing accommodation a tough choice, even when you realize the accommodation is not helping.

You Hate to See Your Child So Upset

This is the most natural feeling in the world. Literally, it is in our nature to be moved by our children's distress. Seeing your child crying, hyperventilating, or begging you for help can place a tremendous emotional burden on you as a parent and can make not accommodating feel cruel and heartless. Your child may also have realized the power of his emotional expression and the result can be even more dramatic displays of distress. Don't think of this as your child being manipulative. It is more fair and accurate to think of it as simple learning and reinforcement: Your child feels very strongly that he needs you to accommodate, and anything making that accommodation more likely to occur will naturally be reinforced. If you have tried not to accommodate in the past, but have given in after your child got very upset, it is almost inevitable that the behavior will repeat, or even get worse in future situations.

This does not mean that your child cannot learn to cope without accommodation. It does mean, however, that in order to achieve that goal, you may need to steel yourself to tolerate some difficult moments. Think of tolerating your child's distress as a lesson you are teaching your child. It is as though you are saying, "This makes me very uncomfortable, but I am able to cope with it because I know I have to"—which is precisely what you want your child to be able to say about her own anxiety: It makes me uncomfortable but I can tolerate it because I know I have to.

You Don't Have Time for This; You Have Other Things to Deal With

This is not as emotional a challenge as the previous example, but it is just as common and just as valid. We all have multiple things to deal with and to accomplish every day, and very often, refusing to accommodate your child will make other goals more difficult to complete. As one mother described:

> Cortney hates to go upstairs by herself. At first it was only at night, after dark, but recently it is anytime. If she needs something from upstairs, she'll get one of us to go with her, or at least one of her brothers. This morning we were rushing to leave for school when we realized Cortney had left her backpack upstairs. I told her to go get it but of course I knew what she would say. When she insisted I go with her, I knew I had a choice: I could go with her and get the backpack. Or I could spend half an hour arguing with her about it, after which maybe she would go by herself, but she and her brothers would definitely be late for school, and I would be late for work. I went with her.

You have probably experienced similar dilemmas as a parent of an anxious child. You can refuse to accommodate and everything will grind to a halt, or you can go along and get through this moment, even though you understand the accommodation is ultimately not helping. If you have made the same choice as Cortney's mom, don't blame yourself. Remember, almost all parents accommodate their anxious children some of the time, and the need to keep a household running is a key reason for this.

This is why it is important not to try to remove all accommodations at once. Having a plan, preparing for challenges, putting the necessary supports in place to deal with them, and then sticking to your plan consistently, are the keys to overcoming the problem. This book will help you make that plan and will suggest some solutions that have worked for other parents. Perhaps at first you will choose to focus only on accommodations that happen after school hours. Or perhaps after mapping out and monitoring your accommodation for a week or two, you will realize there is someplace better to start. For now, cut yourself some slack and remember that nobody can make the perfect choice every time.

Your Child Becomes Angry When You Don't Accommodate, Sometimes Even Aggressive

Many people assume that anxious children are meek or always compliant. This is far from the truth. Children with anxiety or OCD can be just as aggressive as any other child, and with the proper motivation, they will pull out all the stops to achieve what they want. Nothing motivates an anxious child like the need to ensure ongoing accommodation by parents. In a survey of experts in the treatment of OCD, for example, we found that 75% described their young patients as being coercive and forceful in their demands for accommodation. Physical violence, verbal aggression, breaking things, and other forms of disruptive behavior were commonly reported. It is best not to think of this as bad behavior, and it does not signal a negative character trait in the child. If your child becomes aggressive when you do not accommodate, that probably means that she believes she cannot cope without the accommodation. It also might indicate that these kinds of behaviors have worked successfully in the past, in getting you to accommodate. Because disruptive behaviors are so commonly reported by parents of anxious children, Chapter 12 covers how to cope with aggressive behaviors when accommodation is being reduced.

Not Accommodating Just Makes the Anxiety Worse

Here again we need to focus on the slightly longer term. Not the *really* long term, just the *slightly longer* term. It is very likely true that your child will seem more anxious if you do not accommodate. But if you are able to persist consistently, she will likely start to feel less anxious within a short time. The most difficult thing for the child is coming to terms with the idea that you actually will not be accommodating. A lot of her initial response will be driven by the belief that she can still get you to accommodate. Once your child learns that you are not going to accommodate, she will start to realize that she can cope on her own. When that happens you will likely see her anxiety decrease, and the requests for accommodation will go down as well.

What Will Your Child Think? That You Don't Care?

Your child has known you for a long time. If you are reading this book, you surely love your child and want her to feel better. And your child knows that. We do not judge our parents' love based on specific moments in which we do or do not get what we want. Your child may accuse you of not loving her and that can be extremely difficult for any parent to hear. But saying, "You don't love me" is not the same as not feeling loved. Keep in mind that *children do not feel loved because they get what they want. They feel loved because they get what they need* (and not every time, just often enough).

Helping your child to understand your actions and the changes you are making, is an important aspect of this program. You do not need your child to agree with your actions, but you can take steps to ensure that regardless of her agreement, she knows you are acting out of love and because you are determined to help her.

Chapter 7 describes steps you can take, even before you start removing any accommodations, to express your support for your child and to set the stage for the steps you will be taking to help.

Accommodation and Siblings

Parents are not the only ones in a family who are impacted by the presence of a highly anxious child. All family members, including siblings, are likely to experience this impact at some level. Sometimes the impact on siblings is major and pronounced, and other times it may be more subtle, but it is likely that your child's anxiety is having at least some effect on the other members of your household.

One way that a child's anxiety can impact siblings is by causing you to devote time and resources to help your anxious child, leaving you less free for your other children. There's no need to feel guilty or ashamed about this! Being the parent of a child with a difficulty almost inevitably means devoting extra time and resources to coping with the problem. Whether dealing with time, money, energy, or attention, your resources are limited. There are only so many hours in the day, and we all have to budget our time just as we have to budget our income. Parents of children with chronic or serious physical illness often have to spend tremendous resources on helping their child to get well, and the same thing can apply to parents of children with psychological and emotional problems.

Even the time you devote to working through this book (and the cost of purchasing it) are resources you are devoting to helping your anxious child, rather than perhaps helping another child with homework. The good news is that as you work through this book, you will likely be *reducing* the overall time consumed by your child's anxiety. Family accommodation is usually the thing that takes up the most time in coping with a child's anxiety. As you learn to reduce the accommodation, you may find that you have more time to devote to other needs, including those of your anxious child's siblings and your own self-care.

Siblings of anxious children, whether or not they also are prone to elevated levels of anxiety, very often get pulled in to accommodating their sibling in a variety of ways. In some cases these are accommodations that siblings do willingly, perhaps not even realizing that they are accommodating their brother's or sister's anxiety. For example,

Chloe was eight years old and scared to shower alone. Whenever it was time for a shower, she would ask her younger sister, Megan, "Do you want to hear a story?" Megan loved Chloe's stories and was always eager to sit on the stool next to the tub and listen to Chloe.

Chloe's anxiety was impacting her younger sister, who did not see the behavior as a sign of anxiety and was happy with the result (more attention from her older sister). In other cases accommodating siblings are much more aware that their sibling is frightened or worried, but may still be willing to accommodate her to help her feel better, or may simply not mind the accommodation.

Things can be more difficult, however, when the need to accommodate a sibling causes distress or leads to anger, embarrassment, or resentment over time. For example,

- if a family regularly has to skip social events, or
- has to leave movies in the middle, or
- cannot have guests over to the house, or
- parents cannot attend a child's sporting events because of another sibling's anxiety, or
- when arguments about accommodation seem to always spoil things that were supposed to be fun.

Accommodations that are forcefully imposed by an anxious child on their sibling, against that sibling's will, can be particularly problematic. Anxious children and adolescents often will resort to even aggressive coercion in their attempts to ensure that their anxiety is not triggered.

Joss was 12 years old and very concerned about contamination from germs. His twin sister Lindy was used to Joss's fears and did her best not to do anything that would set him off. She was careful to keep her things away from his and patiently answered his questions about whether she had washed her hands and whether she felt sick or not. But mealtimes were becoming almost impossible. Joss would get angry if anyone at the table sneezed or coughed, often yelling at the "culprit" to stop spreading germs and making him sick. Lindy tried sitting as far from Joss as she could at family dinners but was not able to escape his anger for long. Joss seemed to come up with a new rule every week, and no matter how

hard she tried, Lindy always seemed to make him angry. When Joss saw
her yawning at dinner one day he exploded with rage, calling her names
and telling her to keep her dirty germy mouth away from everybody
else. Lindy had had enough. She lost her temper and yelled back at him.
"I'm yawning because I'm tired! I'm tired of you! You and your crazy
rules. Who do you think you are anyway? Why do we all have to listen
to you?" Lindy also yelled at her parents, "Why do you let him get away
with this?! Is he the only one who matters around here?!"

The parents in this example were facing a difficult, but not uncommon, dilemma. They recognized that Joss was acting out of his
obsessive-compulsive symptoms and not simply being unpleasant
or domineering. They were acutely aware that Joss imposed even
stricter rules of hygiene on himself (and on them) and that he was
"victim number one" of the obsessive-compulsive problem. They
also knew that his demands were unfair to Lindy and that the strife
this problem was causing was having a very negative effect on the
family atmosphere.

In this book, you will focus primarily on your own accommodations and less on the accommodations that your other children
may be providing. This is for two main reasons:

1. As already noted, this book aims to help you change the behavior of the one person you can control the most, and that
   person is you. Just as you cannot make a plan for your anxious child to stop being anxious or requesting accommodation, because you don't control his feelings or behavior, you
   also cannot make a plan that relies on controlling the behavior
   of your other children. Even if you were to make such a plan,
   there is no guarantee that your child would choose to follow
   it, or would do so consistently, or in the way you intended.

2. When parents try to intervene in changing the behavior of an
   accommodating sibling, the plan often backfires. Your attempt
   to improve the relationship between your two (or more)

children, may well lead them to argue more. Or they may not appreciate your intervention and become even more tightly allied in maintaining the accommodation. Shaping sibling relations is a difficult thing even in the best of situations, and you are likely to achieve much better results in terms of reducing your child's anxiety if you focus on your own behavior.

You Don't Have To!

So what message can parents give to siblings who are engaging in significant accommodation of an anxious brother or sister? I suggest letting your children know that they are not obligated to accommodate. Rather than forbidding the accommodation (unless clearly inappropriate) or trying to enforce a rule of not accommodating, simply let your other children know that you see what is happening and that you want them to know it is not their job to accommodate their sibling. If you give your children permission not to accommodate, they may still choose to continue the behavior, but they will know that they have your support and will likely feel less frustrated or resentful. If your children are accommodating because they know their sibling is anxious and they are trying to help, you can explicitly acknowledge this and praise them for being considerate and understanding. Even if the accommodation is ultimately not helping, it is still a noteworthy and admirable effort that they are making. You probably want all of your children to be kind and considerate of one another and of other people, and it is worthwhile to emphasize their consideration, while also letting them know they are not expected to continue.

As you work on reducing your own accommodation of your anxious child, your other children will be able to see the changes you make, and this can help them to make some changes in their own accommodation. They will see that you believe the way to help your anxious child is by helping him get better at coping without accommodation, and they may choose to do the same.

If your anxious child is forcefully imposing accommodation on his siblings, it is sensible to act to prevent the use of inappropriate coercion, whether it is happening through excessive pestering, verbal aggression, or physical force. Having done that, let your nonanxious children know they are not expected or required to accommodate, and then keep the focus on your own behavior. Once you have successfully reduced your child's anxiety by working through the rest of this book, it is likely that his need for accommodation by siblings will be less of a problem.

In This Chapter You Learned About:

- What family accommodation is
- How to tell if you are accommodating
- Why parents accommodate
- Good and bad accommodation
- Why it's difficult not to accommodate
- Accommodation by siblings

6

Mapping Accommodation

By now you understand the concept of accommodation and how this can be unhelpful in the long term to children with anxiety. You know that accommodations can maintain your child's anxiety over time and make her less likely to confront her fears. You may also be getting better at noticing the accommodations you provide. Because accommodation can be unhelpful to your child and can place a hefty burden on you and the rest of the family, it makes sense to try to accommodate less. Reducing accommodation is an important part of the method described in this book. But before we jump to reducing family accommodation, there are two very important things to do:

1. First, you will need to have a detailed understanding of the accommodations you are currently providing. Even if you have already identified many of these, it is quite likely that there are others you have not thought about. This chapter will help you to create a detailed "accommodation map" to include as many of the accommodations as possible that you or your family have been providing. You'll be updating this map as you continue to work through this book, adding any additional accommodations you become aware of.

2. The second thing to do before starting to reduce accommodation is to have an alternative response for when your child is anxious. Cutting back on the accommodation is likely to be quite a tough thing to do. But it will be much harder if you do

not have a good plan for what to do instead. The alternative to family accommodation is *support*, and in Chapter 7 you will learn what a supportive response to child anxiety is, and how you can be supportive for your own child.

Once you have created a detailed family accommodation map and learned supportive responses that you can use instead of accommodating, you'll be ready to tackle the work of actually reducing your accommodations—and your child will probably soon be much less anxious.

You may be wondering why it is so important to have a detailed map of family accommodation. After all, if you are already aware of some accommodations why not focus on those and deal with any others as they become more apparent? That's a good question, and the answer is that most parents provide many different forms of accommodation, and it is important to make a choice about which to focus on first. This is a key choice for you to make, and like most decisions it will be easier to make the best decision if you have as much information as possible. Some accommodations are better to focus on than others, and in Chapter 8 you will learn some tips for making the choice of which accommodation to reduce first. But knowing as much as possible about the various accommodations you have been making, will mean you have the most options to choose from and will make it more likely that you select the best accommodation to reduce first.

Making Your Accommodation Map

Before going any further, look at Worksheet 4 (Accommodation List) in Appendix A at the end of this book. The worksheet has places for you to write down the accommodations you are already aware of. Take a few minutes to think over your daily life, and write down as many accommodations as come to mind. If you are not sure whether something is an accommodation, ask yourself these questions:

- Is this something I do because of my child's anxiety?
- Does my child become more anxious if I don't do it?
- Do I do the same for my other children, or would I do it for another child?
- Do I feel as though I have no choice but to do this?
- Do most people do this for their children at this age?
- Have I tried to stop it?

If the behavior is something you do because of your child's anxiety, and he becomes more anxious if you don't do it, it is likely that it is an accommodation. Likewise, if you feel as though you have no choice but to do it or you've tried to stop doing it in the past but continued because your child was anxious, it probably is an accommodation. On the other hand, if you do the same for your other, less anxious children, or if it is something that most people do for children of this age, then it may not be an accommodation. If you are still not sure, however, write it down anyway and don't worry about it. It may not end up being the thing you choose to focus on first, but it won't hurt to have it written down with the other accommodations.

Now that you've written down the accommodations that come to mind most easily, it's time to start figuring out what other accommodations you may also be providing. To do this, use Worksheet 5 (Accommodation Map), also located in Appendix A at the end of this book. Worksheet 5 can help you think over your whole day, from when you get up in the morning until the last thing you do at night before falling asleep. Take a memory-stroll down your recent days and think about each part of the day. Ask yourself if there is anything you do differently at that point in the day because of your child's anxiety. If you think of anything that might be an accommodation, write it down. This worksheet also allows you to include accommodations that someone *else* in the family is providing. That could be your partner, one of your child's siblings, or another person in your child's life such as relatives, teachers, coaches, and even your child's friends. It is not uncommon for relatives, friends, and siblings to provide accommodation, and I encourage you to *write down as many accommodations as you can, regardless of who is providing them.* Figure 6.1 shows a sample accommodation map completed by her parents for 9-year-old Reggie.

As you are going through the day, try to imagine the various situations that commonly occur. For example, when you are thinking about the morning, think about where you are in the house during the morning before your child leaves for school. Are you in the kitchen? Or perhaps you're frequently in your child's bedroom? Or maybe you're not home at all, having left already for work. Ask yourself what you are doing during each time period. Are you interacting with your child? Helping her with some task or other? Are you on the phone or busy with work? And try to think about which things might be different if your child were less anxious. Would you be doing anything differently? Would you be in another place altogether? Would you be focused on your own goals and tasks, rather than on your child? Each thing that you do differently because your child is anxious is another possible accommodation. Make sure to include the accommodations that you already noted in Worksheet 4 so that Worksheet 5 will be as complete a list as possible.

Remember that accommodations don't have to be things that you are actively doing because your child is anxious. Oftentimes we accommodate by *not* doing things that we otherwise would do. If you are not doing things because of your child's anxiety, write down those accommodations, too. For example, if you try not to discuss finances with your partner when your child is home because it makes your child stressed or anxious, you can write down that accommodation.

Time of Day	What Happens? Who Is Involved?	Frequency (Tally)
	e.g., Mom serves breakfast with "special" dishes	1 X Day
Morning (getting up, getting dressed, breakfast, going to school)	Parents go upstairs with Reggie and stay while she chooses clothes and gets dressed.	Every day
	Mom drives Reggie to school; Mom waits for social worker to take Reggie to class.	Every day
	Parents answer worry questions about pick-up	Every day
Afternoon (lunch, pick up from school, homework, after-school activities, social activities)	Mom picks Reggie up; Makes sure to be first in line of cars at pick-up.	Every day
	Mom always stays in eyesight at soccer practice.	Twice a week
Evening (dinner, family time, pre-bedtime)	Mom always lets Reggie know what room Mom is in.	Many times per day
	Parents wait for Reggie to finish playing before going upstairs to get Kath ready for bed.	Every evening
Bedtime (getting ready for bed, washing up/showering, going to bed)	Mom or Dad need to be in the bathroom when Reggie is in the shower (sometimes Kath will go with Reggie instead)	Every night
	Mom/Dad lie in bed with Reggie until she falls asleep	Every night
Nighttime	If Reggie wakes up and comes to their bed, Dad will sleep in Reggie's bed	2–3 times per week
	Mom and Dad keep their bedroom door open all night	Every night
Weekend	Mom and Dad make sure that one of them is always with Reggie (don't go out together or leave her with babysitter)	Every weekend (all day)

FIGURE 6.1 Sample Accommodation Map—9-Year-Old Reggie.

It's important to understand that your child does not have to be anxious for you to be providing an accommodation. Many accommodations are preventative, meaning that parents have become used to providing the accommodation because otherwise their child *would* become anxious. They don't need to wait until the child is actually anxious to accommodate, they can prevent the anxiety in advance through the accommodation. Of course, these accommodations don't actually prevent anxiety, and the child is likely to remain anxious overall. Write down all the things you do *because of* your child's anxiety, whether he is anxious in the moment or not. Even if your child is not asking for the accommodation, if it is something you do because you know he will be anxious otherwise, it still counts as an accommodation.

And finally, remember that accommodations are normal, and every parent of a child with anxiety is likely to be providing them. You're not "confessing" to the accommodations as though they were a crime or a sin. Accommodations are the tools you have found to help your child and to get her and the rest of the family through the day. You're writing them down so that you will be able to pick a focus and have as much information as possible, not because accommodations are "bad" things you have done. This also applies to the accommodations that someone else is providing. Your job is not to "catch" them being accommodating, and they are not "guilty" of accommodating. You're just gathering data that will be useful in helping your child to become less anxious.

Once you have gone through your whole day, from morning to night, try the exercise again, and this time, think about the weekends rather than typical work and school days. Weekend days are different than school days. You may spend more (or less) time with your child on the weekend. You are probably doing different things with her. You may go to different places on the weekend, or be around different people. Try to go through the weekend days the same way that you did for the regular days, writing down as many accommodations as possible.

The next step in completing your accommodation map (you're almost done!) is to go over each accommodation you noted on the worksheet and write down how frequently it occurs. Some accommodations happen very frequently, even many times per day. For example, if your child worry-texts you multiple times a day and you respond with a reassuring message, that could be a very frequent accommodation. Other accommodations are much less frequent, whether because the child does not become anxious as frequently or because they relate to situations that occur more rarely. For example, if your child is scared to stay alone at gymnastics class and you hang around so she can see you, the accommodation can only be as frequent as the class. For each accommodation, note whether it happens multiple times a day, once a day, or how many times a week or month. This data on the frequency of the accommodations is also going to be very helpful in choosing a focus for your next steps and deciding which accommodation to reduce first, as discussed in Chapter 8.

Monitoring Accommodation—Keep a Log

Now that you have your accommodation map, it will be much easier for you to keep track of the accommodations you continue to provide in the coming days and weeks. Try to keep a running log of the accommodations, noting each day which accommodations you provided and how many times. You may realize that there are additional accommodations that are not on the list, and you can simply add them to the accommodation map and continue to monitor these as well. Make some copies of your accommodation map (Worksheet 5), or keep a copy electronically, and update your log each day.

You are not yet actively reducing the accommodation, although that is coming soon, so just try to keep track with no need for special changes. Once you start actively reducing the accommodation, the log will be a useful way to keep track of changes in your overall accommodation, alongside the more specific focus on the accommodation you choose to reduce.

In This Chapter You Learned About:

- Starting your accommodation map
- Monitoring your accommodation

7

How Can You Be Supportive?

You've learned all about anxiety and accommodation, and you've taken the time to map out the accommodations you provide for your child. You're now almost ready to start the work of reducing family accommodation and helping your child to become much less anxious. Reducing family accommodation is hard work for you as the parent, but it is also hard for your child, who has probably come to rely a lot on the accommodations and may take many of them for granted. It's as though a kind of unspoken agreement exists between you and your child that you will help her by providing accommodation, and changing that agreement can be a very hard thing for your child to accept. Your child may also have come to believe that accommodation is the only way for her to feel OK, cope with anxiety, and get through the difficult day. This is not the case, and both you and your child will soon see that your child is actually much more able to cope with anxiety than either of you believe possible. However, as long as your child continues to believe that she can only cope with the anxiety through your accommodations, any change will be a difficult challenge for her to overcome. That is why it is so important to not only reduce the accommodation, but to *increase support*.

Support is your way of helping your child cope with the challenge of less accommodation, and it provides you with an alternative way to respond to your child when he is anxious. Without a plan for what to do instead of accommodation, not accommodating can be almost impossible. After all, it may seem as though you have to do something, and without a plan, you will probably realize that you are doing the usual accommodation. Making a plan in advance for how to respond to your child's anxiety means that you won't have to improvise on the spur of the moment. When your child is highly anxious, you will be under stress to help him, and if his anxiety is very visible or dramatic, that stress can be very powerful. But you won't need to improvise, because you will have a plan for how to respond, and that plan is to respond with support!

Support Means Accepting That Your Child Is Really Scared—But Knowing She Can Cope

When responding to a child who is anxious, support means showing your child two things: *acceptance* and *confidence*. It's like a very simple recipe that has only two ingredients, but both ingredients are necessary if the result is going to be supportive. Figure 7.1 provides the formula:

Pretty simple recipe! You are being *supportive* when you respond to your child's anxiety in any way that tells him that you get it, that you understand he is actually anxious. and that you don't judge him for it (*acceptance*), and also shows him you have complete confidence that he is actually able to cope with some anxiety, and that you know he can be OK despite feeling anxious (*confidence*).

FIGURE 7.1 Recipe for support.

Just like you can't make mac and cheese without both macaroni and cheese, you can't be supportive without both acceptance and confidence!

Think about the traps and pitfalls from Chapter 4. Recall how easy it is to fall into the habit of either demanding or protecting when your child is anxious. Support is exactly the opposite:

- **Support is not demanding**: If you are responding to your child in a demanding way, expecting that she not be anxious or that she behaves as though she is not anxious, that is not supportive because you would be missing the ingredient of acceptance. If you are accepting, that means you acknowledge that your child really is anxious, that she can't choose to feel otherwise just because you say so, and that certain things are genuinely hard for her because of the anxiety.
- **Support is not protecting**: On the other hand, if you are responding to your child by protecting her from anxiety, then that is also not being supportive. Here the missing ingredient is confidence. Protection indicates that you don't believe your child is able to cope with anxiety and needs you to protect her from it.

When you put together acceptance and confidence, that's when you are being supportive.

Being supportive does not mean your child will suddenly stop feeling anxious; support is not a magic trick that can make anxiety go away. And you can't fool your child about acceptance. If you say something supportive and expect that now your child won't be anxious, then that's not really acceptance, is it? Actions always speak louder than words. If you say something accepting—but act in a way that shows your child that you don't really accept his anxiety—then your child will probably not feel supported. And it is the same for confidence. Again, your actions speak much louder than words. If you tell your child you believe he can cope with anxiety, but your behavior shows that you don't believe it (e.g., if you follow the supportive statement with accommodation), then your child won't believe that you have confidence in him after all.

Melany and Brody were frustrated with their daughter Dayana, who was 11 years old and in the sixth grade. Since the beginning of the school year, Dayana had been having trouble taking the school bus to school. She was worried about not being able to sit next to her best friend, anxious that she would be teased or picked on by another child, and scared that if she took the bus she would be so upset that her whole school day would be a disaster. Melany and Brody had both tried to talk to her about taking the bus many times. They told her that driving her to school every day was very hard for them and made them late for work. They reminded her that all her friends took the bus and had no problem with it. They tried to ask her if she had actually ever been bullied on the bus and Dayana said she had not, but it didn't matter. Nothing her parents said seemed to help, and each morning the same scene would repeat. Melany and Brody would start the day acting as though they assumed that their daughter was going to take the bus. At some point during breakfast one of them would say something about the school bus coming to pick her up, being careful to use a casual tone of voice as though the topic were completely neutral and not an ongoing problem. Dayana would immediately stop eating and in a tone that was either angry or unhappy, she would say something like, "You know I can't take the bus." The parents would try a while longer to cling to feigned innocence, asking, "Why not?" or "What's the problem?" and Dayana would become increasingly upset. Then the parents would again try to talk her into going, saying whatever they could to make her feel as though she was able to go, or to make clear that she had to go. Dayana would refuse to leave the house for the bus stop, and in the end, one of her parents would drive her to school, only to repeat the same scene the next day. After more than a month, both parents felt they hated schoolday mornings and would wake up dreading the scene at breakfast.

Melany and Brody were trying their best to get their daughter to overcome a fear. They seemed to be saying all the right things but nothing seemed to help. Think about their responses to Dayana and whether they were being supportive. What do you think? Remember the simple recipe of acceptance and confidence. Do you think that Dayana's parents were showing acceptance of her fear? At first, it may seem as though they were accepting. They didn't say anything mean or harsh to her about it, and they didn't tease or make fun of her fear. But reading their words more closely, it seems likely that Dayana did not feel a lot of acceptance. When her parents reminded her that all her friends were able to take the bus, their intention was probably to make her feel as though she could do the same, or to show her that nothing bad had happened to her friends as a result of taking the bus. But saying that none of her friends have this problem is actually a way of saying that Dayana shouldn't have a problem either.

Dayana already knew that her friends took the bus, and she probably felt badly about having a problem that they didn't have. Comparing a child with an anxiety problem to children who don't have the same problem is unlikely to help the child feel better. Would you tell a child with a sprained ankle, "All your friends can run with no problem, why can't you?" Of course you wouldn't; that would be absurd. It makes no sense to expect a child with a problem to be the same as another child without that problem. Children are usually quite sensitive to this kind of comparison, and it rarely feels supportive. Children are particularly attuned to being compared to their own siblings. If you tell your child with anxiety, "Your brother did this at your age," or "Why can't you do it like your sister?" you may be trying to encourage the child, but you are not saying something supportive.

Brody and Melany did another thing, which is common, but not accepting of their daughter's anxiety. They began each weekday by acting as though they had every expectation that Dayana would ride the bus without issue. The parents were not trying to be disingenuous or to deny that Dayana had a problem. Their make-believe expectation that Dayana would ride the bus was simply their way of showing her that they thought she could do it, and it expressed the hope, slim though it was, that the morning could go a different way. They may even have worried that if they assumed Dayana would not go, then it would be harder for her to get back into the habit of going, even if the anxiety were to stop being a problem. There is some sense to this, because children can sometimes find themselves up a tree, unable to admit that they want to change. Melany and Brody may have believed that by acting as though there were no reason for her not to go on the bus, they were giving Dayana an out, an opportunity to simply go on the bus without having to make a big deal out of it.

In actual fact, however, it was a big deal for Dayana, and having her parents act as though there was no reason for her to have difficulty going to school on the bus probably felt false and not accepting. Dayana knew that her parents were aware that she had not taken the bus in many weeks, and she may have felt that by denying the problem, her parents were rejecting the idea that something like taking the school bus can be hard. This kind of denial probably made Dayana feel pretty bad.

How about confidence? Were Melany and Brody showing Dayana confidence, the other ingredient in support? The parents did make efforts to show Dayana that they believed she could go on the bus. They told her so repeatedly, and the statements about how her friends took the bus were intended to show that they thought their daughter also could do it. But remember, actions always speak louder than words. Every morning ended up with one or the other parent driving Dayana to school. By driving her to school, the parents are undermining the message that they believe she is able to cope with the bus. By agreeing to drive her, they are essentially acknowledging that, at least on that day, the child is not able to go after all. When it is followed by the accommodation, the message, "We know you can do it," is transformed into, "We think you should be able to do it (but we realize you can't)."

Of course, Melany and Brody may have felt that they did not have a choice. Dayana needed to get to school one way or the other, and given that they were not able to get her on the bus, they probably felt that the only option was to take her themselves. Even if this were true, it would still undermine the confidence element of support, and, in fact, it may not have been true at all. Because the parents ended up taking her to school each morning, they had no opportunity to find out what Dayana actually was capable of. It may be that if they did not take her, Dayana would have ultimately felt like she was the one with no choice but to get on the bus. Or it may be that she would have missed a day of school, arrived late, or found another means of getting there, such as asking for help from someone else. If she did miss a day, it is possible that having learned that her parents were not going to take her, she would have found the strength to get on the bus. There are many possibilities, but none of them can occur as long as the parents end up taking her each morning.

Soon you will be making your own plans for reducing accommodation, and you will have to face similar challenges. Deciding at what point to give in and provide accommodation, thinking through the possible outcomes (e.g., a child refusing to go to school), and having detailed plans for handling those outcomes, will all help you to reduce the accommodation with as little stress and as much success as possible. In Chapter 9 you will find useful tools to help you make the best plans possible, and in Chapter 12 and Chapter 13 you will learn strategies for coping with difficult situations that can arise while you work on your plan. In the meantime, however, continue practicing being supportive.

Why Is Support So Important?

Having a plan means you won't have to improvise your responses when your child is anxious, and a plan provides you with an alternative response when you begin to reduce the accommodation. Any

plan to respond to your child's anxiety in a way that is not accommodating could do both of these things, so why is it *so important that
your plan be to respond with support*?

Support, for a child who is highly anxious, is a particularly useful
message. It combines the two most important things that can help
a child who is anxious (acceptance and confidence). Many children
with anxiety feel misunderstood by others, including their parents,
who don't experience the same levels of anxiety, or who don't get
anxious about the same things. Feeling misunderstood can be very
lonely. Just as importantly, if your child does not have the sense that
you understand his difficulty, then he is probably going to be very
skeptical about any advice or help you try to give. After all, why get
help from someone who doesn't understand or accept the problem?
When you show your child acceptance, you are telling him that you
get it, that you *do* understand how hard the anxiety can be for him.
This makes it more likely that he will be open to hearing the second
part of the supportive message—the confidence.

Children with high levels of anxiety often feel helpless and vulnerable in the face of the overwhelming anxiety they experience.
They have probably learned that the way to cope with anxiety is to
rely on avoidance and accommodation, and they may not believe
they are able to cope any other way. When you show your child confidence, you are indicating to him that he is not helpless, weak, or
vulnerable. You are telling him that he is strong! Your child might
not believe it right away, but seeing that you consistently view him
as strong and capable, even though you know how anxious he is, will
start to add up. Over time, your child will come to view himself as
stronger than he did before, and once he begins to feel that way, the
anxiety is already on the way out!

Believing that you can't cope with anxiety is the biggest part
of having an anxiety problem or disorder. You may think that your
child's problem is mostly that she has too much anxiety, and in one
sense you are correct. But in another very important and real sense,
your child's problem is actually not *how much* anxiety she has, but

how willing she is to be anxious. Two children with similar levels of anxiety are not necessarily going to have the same level of anxiety problem. Why not? Because one of those children may be more willing to experience anxiety than the other.

This is a subtle and important point, and it may be easier to explain if we think about other things we try to avoid, not necessarily because of anxiety. Everyone wants to avoid physical discomfort as much as possible. Almost no one likes discomfort or pain, but different people have different attitudes toward pain. Some treat it as an awful thing to be avoided at all costs, while others accept that they will sometimes experience pain and hope it won't be too bad or last too long.

It's the same for other kinds of discomfort. Most children (and adults) dislike throwing up. Vomiting is unpleasant and can be painful, and most of us would rather avoid it if possible. But it's not how painful the vomiting is that determines whether a child is determined never to throw up or whether he simply prefers not to. It is more about the *attitude* he has toward the discomfort than about the level of actual objective discomfort. Consider two children who both get sick and throw up, and imagine that the experience is identical for both of them: They have the same level of discomfort, it lasts the same amount of time, and they both have the identical bad taste in their mouths at the end. Are both of those children going to be equally determined never to throw up again? Not necessarily. One child, Rosie, may think, "That was horrible, and I never ever ever want to go through that again, ever!" The other child, Hannah, may simply think, "Yuck!" Or even, "Yuck, but at least I feel a bit better now." These two children will behave differently in the future. Rosie, the child who is determined never to throw up again, might begin to take special precautions, such as eating only certain "safe" foods, staying away from people who have been ill, and eating very slowly, all in order to ensure that she doesn't throw up again. Hannah, who simply thought "yuck," probably won't go to such lengths. Remember, the actual experience of throwing up was the same for both girls, so why are they now behaving differently? Because of the thoughts they have *about* throwing up.

It is the same with anxiety, fears, worries, and stress. Can you see how it is not necessarily the level of your child's anxiety that is most important in determining whether it will be a problem in his life? If your child has an anxiety problem, it is likely that at some level he is trying very hard not to feel anxious. This is entirely natural. In fact, keeping us away from the things that make us anxious is the whole reason we have an anxiety system in the first place. But when a child becomes determined not to experience anxiety, he is likely to start taking extra precautions, staying away from things that are not actually a danger and avoiding normal situations in ways that impede his daily functioning.

The reason that some children are more determined not to experience anxiety than others has a lot to do with the child's beliefs about her own anxiety. Even though children might not be aware of those beliefs, the beliefs are there and they matter just the same. If your child believes she is weak, vulnerable, or helpless to cope with anxiety, then she is going to want to avoid feeling anxious if at all possible. Likewise, if your child believes that anxiety, once it has been triggered, will never go away on its own and will only go down through avoidance or accommodation, then, of course, she is going to do everything in her power to avoid becoming anxious. And if she does become anxious, she will try very hard to get you to accommodate, so that she can feel better.

We know it is *not true* that anxiety can go down only through avoidance or accommodation. In fact, anxiety will always diminish on its own, if we just give it time. But if your child does not believe this, and thinks he will be completely overwhelmed or stuck with the anxiety, then naturally he will try very hard to stay away from anything that can make him anxious. Ironically, trying to stay away from anxiety is the surest way to actually feel anxious. Why is that? When your child thinks of anxiety as a terrible feeling he is powerless to cope with, then even small things take on oversized meaning.

If all anxiety is bad, then every moment has the potential to be catastrophic, and your child needs to always be on the lookout for any sign that anxiety is coming. That's sure to keep him anxious!

You can't directly change your child's beliefs about anxiety. Teaching and explaining are usually not powerful enough to change a child's beliefs, and your child may not be open to hearing from you about what she should think or believe. But you do have the power to *indirectly* impact your child's beliefs about anxiety. This is why the confidence element of support is so important and also why protective responses can maintain the child's anxiety. When your child looks at you and sees that you are completely confident that she can cope, it will have an impact on her and on what she believes. When your child sees that you are willing for her to feel anxious some of the time, she will also be able to become less afraid of feeling anxious. As her confidence grows, her need to avoid feeling anxious will get smaller. And a child who is willing to feel anxious some of the time is well on the way to not having an anxiety problem at all.

As a parent—not only the parent of an anxious child, but as a parent in general—you are the mirror that your child looks into to see who he is. The things you reflect to your child will shape his understanding of himself. When your child tries to be amusing, he looks at you to know if he is funny. If you laugh at his jokes and show him that he is funny, then he will probably believe that he can be funny. If, on the other hand, you always scowl at his attempts at humor, your child may learn that he is not funny. It's the same for how children understand their own anxiety. If your child looks at you and the reflection he sees of himself is a weak child who can't cope with anxiety, then he will probably come to believe that is true. But if you show him through your words, and more importantly, through your actions, that you know your child is strong enough to cope with some anxiety, then he can learn that instead.

There is one more reason why support, in particular, is the best alternative to accommodation, and why you should practice being supportive even before you begin to reduce the accommodations. Practicing support will provide a positive framework for your child to understand the changes you are going to make to the accommodations. When children rely heavily on accommodation, they can become confused when parents start to withdraw it. Your child may even believe that you are reducing the accommodation for reasons that are completely different from the actual reasons. For example, if your child knows that the accommodation is inconvenient or unpleasant for you, then she might think you are stopping accommodation because you are tired of it, or because you are no longer willing to help her. This is completely the opposite of the truth. You know that you will be reducing the accommodation precisely in order to help your child. And you know that it is not because you are tired of the accommodation (although that might very well be). In fact, it is likely that in the very short term reducing the accommodation will be at least as much work as providing it. You know these things, but your child may not! By preceding the changes in accommodation with an increase in support, you are providing your child with a way of understanding the changes you will be making. If you show your child that you understand and accept the anxiety, and that you believe in your child's ability to cope, then it will be easier for your child to see the change in accommodation as a means of helping him to get better. This doesn't mean he will accept the change easily, but it does make it far less likely that he will misunderstand your actions.

Are You Being Supportive?

Use Worksheet 6 (Things You Say) located in Appendix A at the end of this book, to write down the things you say to your child when she is anxious. You may even want to ask for some help with this task because we are not always the best at remembering what we say, and what we actually say is often different from what we mean or plan to say. You can ask your partner for help and encourage them to tell you openly what things they hear you saying to your child when she is feeling anxious. You can even ask your child, who is probably the best expert on what you say to her! You may also want to refer back to the sentences you wrote on Worksheet 2 (Parenting Traps) and include some of those as well. Write down on Worksheet 6 the phrases and statements you use to respond to your child's anxiety. Then try to indicate for each statement whether it includes the key elements of acceptance and confidence. Don't worry if not everything you say is very supportive. No parent is able to be supportive all the time, even after learning about support and what it involves. Just try to look for each of the ingredients and note whether they are present in the things you say.

Figure 7.2 presents examples of statements that parents sometimes make to their child, or about their child, with notations for whether these statements include the elements of acceptance and confidence. The last few rows are blank so that you can decide what you think: Do the statements show acceptance? Confidence?

Practice Being Supportive

Take a look at the things you wrote down on Worksheet 6. You can pick some of the phrases you wrote and try to change them to make them more supportive following the simple recipe of:

Acceptance + Confidence = Support

If your statement was accepting but did not show your child that you also have confidence that he can cope with anxiety, try adding a confidence statement to go with the acceptance. You can add something like, "I know you can handle it," or "I know you'll be OK," or you can come up with your own words that express your confidence in your child's ability to tolerate anxiety.

Statement	Acceptance	Confidence
You just have to power through.	—	✓
I can't be dealing with this right now.	—	—
I get it, it's not easy for everyone.	✓	—
Enough is enough!	—	—
You're fine!		✓
You've always been a worrier.	✓	—
You're going to have to learn to handle things.	—	—
I wish you would just suck it up.	—	—
Why can't you be more like your sister.	—	—
I'll help you now, but next time I won't.		
Life doesn't all revolve around you, you know.		
It's hard but you can do it.		
There's nothing out there to be scared of.		
When are you going to grow up already?		
It's hard for me, too, but I manage and I'm sure you can as well.		

FIGURE 7.2 Things parents say to anxious children—Are they supportive?

You don't have to express confidence that your child actually *will* choose to cope better or face his fear or do something that is difficult. After all, you don't have control over what your child will actually do. He may hear the supportive statement and still not feel able to cope with the anxiety, but this doesn't mean that the supportive statement is wrong! It just means that your child is not ready, or has not yet found the strength to cope. If you continue working through this book, your child will probably be less anxious soon, and you will be able to see the changes in his behavior. In the meantime, let's keep the focus on what *you* are doing—not on what your child is doing.

The supportive statement is a statement about you, not your child. When you express confidence in your child, you are simply stating what you believe, not what she will do. Once you see it that way, it may be easier for you to express the confidence. If you think of confidence as confidence in what your child will do, then the supportive statement may feel dishonest. After all, how confident can you actually be in what your child is going to do? But if you keep the focus on you, and remember that you are telling your child that *you* believe she can tolerate anxiety, then the statement can be completely honest and accurate regardless of what your child does.

Referring again to Worksheet 6, if you notice that most of the things you say express your confidence in your child, but do not express acceptance, then try adding an accepting statement to the message. It might be easier to say the accepting part first, before the confidence part, so that your child knows that when you express confidence, it is not because you don't understand his difficulty. But the order does not really matter, and you can say it however feels best to you. Every parent and family have their own style of communication, their own internal "family language" for how to talk about things. You can try different ways of saying it and see what feels best to you.

Don't worry if at first the supportive statements feel less natural to you than what you were used to saying. That's very normal and reflects the fact that what you are doing now is different from what you did in the past. Change always feels less natural at first, but stick with it and pretty soon being supportive will be second nature to you.

Figure 7.3 provides examples using statements from Figure 7.2, of how a statement that is missing part of support can be changed to be a supportive statement with both acceptance and confidence:

Using Worksheet 7 (Supportive Statements) located in Appendix A at the end of this book, try to change some of your statements from Worksheet 6 into more supportive statements. Practice saying them a few times. You can even role-play with your partner or a friend, so that these statements start to feel more familiar. Pick one or two

Old Statement	Acceptance	Confidence	New Statement	Acceptance	Confidence
You just have to power through.		✓	*It's hard, but you have the power to get through!*	✓	✓
I get it, it's not easy for everyone.	✓		*I get that it's hard, but I'm sure you can cope.*	✓	✓
You're fine!		✓	*I know it's really hard now, but you're going to be fine.*	✓	✓
You've always been a worrier.	✓		*You feel worried, but it's OK to feel that way.*	✓	✓
You're going to have to learn to handle things.			*Anxiety is uncomfortable, but you can handle it.*	✓	✓
I'll help you now, but next time I won't.	✓?		*I know you feel like you need my help, but I believe in you.*	✓	✓

FIGURE 7.3 Making statements more supportive.

statements that you like and that you think will be a good fit for the situations you encounter with your child. Plan to say them next time you see that your child is feeling anxious. Remember, it's OK for the statements not to feel completely natural at first.

Your child may find the new supportive statements to be surprising, different, or even funny. She may wonder why you are responding differently than in the past. That's a natural reaction, and you can simply tell her that you have been thinking and working on how you respond to her anxiety because you want to help her as best you can.

From now on, try to use the supportive statements as often as possible. Don't worry about repeating the same things over and over, that's OK! It is important for your child to hear you being supportive as often as possible. When your child asks you a worry question, is seeking reassurance, or is struggling with anxiety, try to make a supportive statement. At first you may find it hard to remember to use supportive statements. You may realize only after the situation has passed that you were planning to respond with support. Don't feel badly; just try again next time. If you realize during an interaction that you are falling back on your more typical responses, you can just pause for a second and say something like, "Actually, you know what I really want to say is . . . ." With practice it will get easier to use supportive statements, and you may be surprised at how your child responds. You already know not to expect the supportive statements to work magic, and they most likely will not. But your child may find ways to show you how meaningful the support is. Just doing something another way creates the opportunity for the interaction to go differently. By changing the script of the usual interaction with your child, you are in turn giving him the opportunity to do something different as well.

Of course, your child at first may have a less positive reaction to the supportive statement. Some children seem to reject the support in the beginning. It is common for a child to say something like, "No, you don't understand at all," or "If you know how hard it is, why do you think I can do it?!" or "Stop saying that!" or even, "You sound like a psychologist now, who taught you to say that?" You don't have to try to make your child accept the support. Remember, the focus is on what *you* are doing, and the supportive statement is about you not your child. Children can benefit from hearing expressions of support regardless of how they react.

Did you ever give your child a compliment that he rejected? Children often push back against compliments and praise. Maybe you've said something like, "You did a great job!" and your child reacted with, "No I didn't!" Or perhaps you said something like, "You look so nice today," and your child said, "No I don't, I look terrible!" Maybe you yourself have responded to compliments this same way. Does that mean you don't want to be praised, or that you should stop complimenting your child because he didn't accept the compliment with grace? Of course not. Children who push back and have a hard time accepting a compliment still need to hear positive things about themselves. But there is no point in getting into an argument over it. If you give your child a compliment and he doesn't accept it, you're far better off saying something like, "Well, that's what I think," than trying to force him to agree with the praise. The fact that he doesn't accept the praise doesn't mean that he doesn't care what you think, or even that he doesn't cherish your good words. The same thing goes for support in response to child anxiety. If your child reacts negatively to the support, that doesn't mean it has no value, or that she isn't hearing it, or that she doesn't cherish your support. Keep being supportive, and let your child respond in the way that she does.

Spend a week or two showing your child a lot of support by making as many supportive statements as possible. For now it is OK if you continue to provide accommodation; just make sure to use the supportive statements. So, for example, if your child is asking you to accompany him to bed and that is something you have been doing until now, you can still go with him. You could say, "I get that you're feeling scared about being alone, but I know you can cope with being scared." Then if your child still wants you to come with him, you can do so. Once you've practiced using the supportive statements for a week or two, it will be time to start focusing on the next step—reducing the accommodation. The first step in that process is to choose which accommodation you will be changing. The next chapter will help you decide which accommodation to reduce first.

In This Chapter You Learned About:

- Support for anxious children
- Support = Acceptance + Confidence
- Why support is so important
- Whether you are being supportive
- Practicing to make supportive statements to your child

8

Which Accommodation Should You Reduce First?

This chapter will help you pick a good target accommodation on which to focus as you begin the process of reducing family accommodation of your child's anxiety. For some parents this might be an easy choice, whether because there are not many accommodations, or because one stands out as the obvious choice. But it's likelier that you will have identified a number of accommodations, and the choice may not be clear or simple.

Look over your accommodation map (Worksheet 5 in Appendix A) and the logs you have been keeping of the ways you accommodate your child's anxiety. Once more, think about whether there are accommodations you have not listed, and, if so, add those to the map. Then read through the rest of this chapter and choose the accommodation you think is the best target to take on first.

Why Pick an Accommodation At All?

If accommodations are unhelpful and can maintain your child's anxiety, why not try to reduce them all? Why not stop accommodating altogether? One reason is that you may find it impossible to stop accommodating all at once. There may be too many accommodations, and even if you could stop them all, doing so would likely make the process needlessly difficult for your child. Adjusting to change in a parent's behavior is not easy for a child, and reducing one accommodation at a time will allow your child to adjust to the new behavior without being overwhelmed.

Most parents who try to stop many accommodations at the same time, will find that it is almost impossible to stick to that goal consistently. You may find that instead of a consistent change in one particular area, you end up with very inconsistent changes across a whole lot of areas. Your child's anxiety will improve more rapidly if you are able to be consistent in one area, even if you continue to accommodate in other ways, than if you behave inconsistently across a variety of situations.

Being inconsistent in reducing the accommodation also has other disadvantages. If you are inconsistent, that is, sometimes accommodating and sometimes not, then something is going to be determining which times you accommodate and which times you don't. What is that something going to be? It won't be your plan, because your plan is not to accommodate at all. Instead, what will determine whether you accommodate is more likely to be something such as, what mood you happen to be in, how tired or energetic you happen to feel, how much time you have at the moment, or how you happen to feel about your child right then. It makes sense that these things would influence whether or not you accommodate, but they are not at all helpful.

If you accommodate only when you are feeling refreshed (and therefore not when you're tired), the message your child learns is not, "I know you can cope without accommodation," but rather, "I know you do need me to accommodate, but right now I don't have the energy for you." Or, if you accommodate based on how you feel about your child, for example, not accommodating when she's annoyed you or has misbehaved, then the message becomes, "I am not going to help you because I'm mad at you." Likewise, if you accommodate when you have the time but not when you're busy or rushed, your child may get the message, "I would help you, but I'm too busy right now."

What these messages have in common is that they are not supportive. A supportive message tells the child, "By not accommodating I *am* helping you," but your child is only likely to see the change in accommodation this way if you are able to be as consistent as possible. If you don't accommodate regardless of whether you are tired, annoyed, busy, or upset, then your child will see that you are acting this way because you believe it is the right thing to do. Your child may not agree with you, but she will know that it is what you believe, and it will be easier for her to come to terms with the new plan. A child who thinks you are not helping her because you are too busy with other things is likely to resist the change much longer than a child who knows you are acting in accordance with what you think is best for her.

Another disadvantage of inconsistency in reducing accommodation is that your child has no way of knowing when you will accommodate and when you won't. If you sometimes accommodate, even though you have told him that you won't, then your child has no choice but to try his luck and find out whether you will accommodate this time or not. This will maintain your child's efforts at getting you to accommodate much longer. In other words, if there is no way for your child to predict when you will provide the accommodation, then he will treat every situation as one in which you might. This is even more true if you sometimes start off refusing to accommodate, but then end up accommodating after all. It's natural for this to happen if you are trying to reduce all the accommodations at once.

In Chapter 9 you will make a very detailed and specific plan for how you are going to change your behavior around the accommodation you choose to reduce. This is another good reason to have just one accommodation to focus on at a time. It wouldn't be possible for you to have such a detailed plan for every accommodation, and your plan would probably end up being something general, such as *don't accommodate*. But *don't accommodate* is not a plan at all; it is merely a goal. The difference between a goal and plan is that a plan will provide details and specifics on when and how your behavior will change. What will you do instead? How will you explain it to your child? How will you respond to your child when she reacts to not being accommodated by you? The plan will help the process to go much more smoothly and is only possible if you choose a specific accommodation.

There is yet another good reason to choose one accommodation and focus on it. If you are successful in reducing one or two accommodations, by focusing on them one at a time, you will probably discover that you don't have to take on the others. Why is this? By successfully reducing those first one or two accommodations, you are helping your child's anxiety to improve! Reducing accommodation actually reduces child anxiety. As your child's anxiety diminishes, and he becomes stronger, less vulnerable to anxiety, and more confident in his ability to tolerate some anxiety in his life, his need for those other accommodations is also likely to go down. Just as anxiety and avoidance can be generalized over time—leading to more avoidance of more things—coping also can be generalized. Your child will be learning to cope with anxiety and will likely apply his newfound ability in other situations, making it easier for him to cope without accommodations, even if you have not targeted them directly.

What's a "Good" Accommodation to Reduce?

As you look over the items on your accommodation map, consider these suggestions for picking a good target accommodation to reduce.

Pick Something that Happens Frequently

Choose an accommodation that occurs regularly, rather than infrequently. Choosing something frequent will give you many opportunities to practice "not accommodating" and will give your child many chances to experience "overcoming anxious feelings" on her own. A good target is something that happens multiple times per week, or even per day. You may feel there is another accommodation—something that happens much less often and is a bigger problem for your child. For example, if your child is very anxious during fire drills in school and you have been keeping her out of school on days with fire drills, this might seem like an important target to address. But consider how hard it will be for you to practice this change. Fire drills don't take place that often, and you have no way to increase their frequency. Unless you are the school principal, you don't get to decide when the school practices fire drills. Choose something that happens more often, and your child will have many more opportunities to overcome her anxiety. In the end, you may decide that you still need to change your behavior around the fire drills, and that is OK. But you also may realize your child is no longer that anxious about them, because you've been able to reduce her anxiety by working on other, more frequent targets.

Pick Something You Can Control

Remember that reducing accommodation is all about changing *your* behavior, not someone else's, and this includes your child. Ask yourself whether the target you are considering is really something that you do, or don't do, or whether you are actually trying to get your child's behavior to change. For example, what if your child is afraid of being alone and follows you around the house from room to room? The important question is, "What do *you* do that helps your child to be near you?" If you always let him know when you leave a room, or keep open doors that you would otherwise shut, then those are accommodations that you can control and which it makes sense to take on as a target. But if you go about your business as you otherwise would, and it is only your child's behavior that is different because of the anxiety, then you are not accommodating in that situation. Your child is displaying anxious behavior, of course, but it is your child's behavior and not something you can directly control.

You should be able to state the change you are going to make to your own behavior in a way that does not involve any change on the part of your child. For example, "I am going to stop keeping the bathroom door open when I shower," or, "I am going to stop answering the phone when I'm at work," or, "I am not going to double-check the front door lock with my child." Notice how none of these statements mention any change to your child's behavior. If you are not able to state the target accommodation in this way (with "I am" or "I am not" statements), then it is likely that you are considering a target that is outside of your control, and it's best if you think of a different target instead.

Pick Something that Bothers You

You are more likely to be determined and resolute in reducing the accommodation if you feel that the accommodation is a problem for you as well as your child. The main reason for reducing accommodation is to help your child get better, but it will be easier to stick with a plan if removing that accommodation also improves your life. For example, many parents provide accommodation by sleeping next to their child who is anxious about sleeping alone or who has difficulty falling asleep if her parent is not there. Some parents find this disturbing or aggravating and long to be able to get a good night's sleep without their child next to them, or to spend some quality time with their partner. For these parents, restoring the privacy of their own bed can be a good target. Other parents enjoy the closeness of having their child nearby at night, or simply do not feel strongly about it one way or the other. If your child sleeps next to you, and you don't mind, it might be harder for you to make a change that leads to some difficult or sleepless nights.

Table 8.1 contains examples of accommodations for various domains of anxiety that could be good targets because (1) they are happening frequently, (2) they are behaviors parents control and can choose to change, and (3) they are causing parents some significant interference.

Which Accommodations are Not Good to Focus On?

This next section explains why some target accommodations should not be your first choice when figuring out what to reduce.

Is It Really About the Anxiety?

Anxious children are not *only* anxious children and not everything you do for your child is directly related to anxiety. For example, if you prepare special foods for your child, it may because she is anxious about eating and it causes her to be very picky, or it could be that your child just happens to prefer something specific. Even if you would like to stop preparing the special food, it's best for now to focus on an accommodation that you are confident stems from your child's anxiety.

Here is another example: Anxious children may be accommodated in their homework, often by having a parent sit next to them while they work, check their work repeatedly for errors, or help them with work that they are actually capable of doing on their own. There could also be other reasons, however, for a parent to spend time on their child's homework. Children with learning difficulties or attention deficit problems also may require extra help with their

TABLE 8.1 Good Target Accommodations are Frequent, Controllable, and Interfering

Anxiety Domain	Good Target Accommodation to Reduce
Separation Anxiety	Parents get up extra early each day because child wakes up and wants to be downstairs in the morning but is anxious about being on a different floor of the house from parents
	Parents play "Marco Polo" to let child know where they are in the house
	Parents lie in bed with child at nighttime
Obsessive-Compulsive	Parents repeatedly check food expiration dates and reassure child that food is not expired
	Parents do not park car next to black cars (the color black triggers child's obsessive thoughts)
	Parents hug child repeatedly until the pressure of the hug feels "just right"
Social Anxiety	Father never wears shorts when outside with child because child is embarrassed
	Parents speak in place of child in various settings
	Parents do not speak on the phone when child is in the room
Generalized Anxiety	Parents answer repeated questions about the future and reassure child she will be OK
	Parents do not read the newspaper at home because of child's worry
Phobias	Parents check child's room for spiders each night
	Parents ask to excuse child from health class because of fear of blood and medical equipment or content
Panic and Agoraphobia	Parents pick child up from school when child is feeling panic symptoms
	Parents avoid malls and other crowded places
Food and Eating	Parents check restaurant menus with child before going to ensure there is an "acceptable" food
	Parents prepare special meals for child

homework, and some children may be unwilling to do the work at all, leading parents to spend a lot of time prompting or cajoling them to do it, or supervising them so they stay on task. Try to make sure you are choosing to focus on an anxiety accommodation, and leave the other things for another day.

Don't Mix Goals

A "mixed goal" is when reducing the accommodation intersects with another objective you have as a parent. For example,

- Your child may have difficulty being apart from you and may not want to spend time in his room alone. Helping him to overcome this problem is a good objective (although it's not yet a target, because it only describes the child's behavior and not yours), but it can become intertwined with other objectives. You may want your child to be able to be alone in his room *so that he can clean it up.* A clean room is a good thing, but a messy room is (probably) not an anxiety symptom.
- Many children resist going to bed and want to stay up later. Your child may be resisting bedtime because of a fear of being alone in bed, and working on your child's ability to cope with being in bed alone could be a good goal. But your child could be showing "normal" resistance to ending the day and going to bed.
- Another example relates to getting ready for school in the morning. Many children procrastinate in the morning, taking a long time to get ready to leave for school. The procrastination can reflect a child's anxiety, for example, about school or about making clothing choices. But it can also reflect other non-anxiety-related things, such as difficulty with organization or a general attitude toward school and tasks.

Do Both Parents Agree?

If you and your partner are working through this book together, consider whether both of you think that the accommodation you are considering is an important or useful goal. If the accommodation is one that you disagree on, try to think of one that you both agree would be a good thing to reduce. Taking on a target that becomes a source of disagreement or conflict in your relationship will probably make the process harder.

Table 8.2 lists examples of accommodations that do not make great targets and includes explanations as to why.

Choose Your Target!

Now that you've learned all about what makes an accommodation a good (or a poor) target for your first plan, it's time to make a choice. Remember to choose something that is frequent, causes you some meaningful interference, is related to the anxiety, and is something you can control. Take one more look at your accommodation map and choose the target you think is best. If you are working with your partner, talk about it together and make sure that you are in agreement.

The next steps will be to come up with a specific plan for how your behavior is going to change, and to let your child know in advance so she understands what you're doing and isn't surprised by the change in your behavior. In Chapter 9 you will make your own plan for reducing accommodation, and in Chapter 10 you will make a plan for sharing this information with your child. While you're working on your plan, keep up the supportive statements and continue to monitor your accommodation, now focusing specifically on the target accommodation, rather than on all the accommodations.

TABLE 8.2 Examples of Poor Accommodation Targets

Anxiety Domain	Not a Good Target Accommodation	Why Not?
Separation Anxiety	Parents would like to plan a weekend getaway but have postponed because of child's separation anxiety	A one-time trip will not provide enough practice opportunity
	Parents give child a reward if child stays in bed alone	Providing a reward is not an accommodation
Obsessive-Compulsive	Child washes hands many times each day	It's a child behavior, not a parental accommodation
	Parents will not allow more than two hours of screen time	Not an anxiety or accommodation target
	Parents will stop all accommodation	Not specific; not likely to be implemented consistently
Social Anxiety	Parents will only speak in place of child if child is very anxious	Inconsistent and sends a message that child cannot cope when anxiety is higher
Generalized Anxiety	Instead of answering repeated questions, parents will calmly provide details about how diseases are transmitted	Replaces one reassurance with another
	Child will only be allowed three phone calls a day	Not a parent behavior (could be changed to how many times parents will answer calls)
Phobias	Child will gradually practice exposure to dogs, starting with very small ones	Not an accommodation target or a parent behavior
Panic and Agoraphobia	Mother will pick up child from school if feeling panic, but father will not leave work to come pick up	Maintains the accommodation; creates conflict between parents
Food and Eating	Mother will stop preparing special foods each day; Father will only provide preferred foods	These parents disagree about the target and the plan

In This Chapter You Learned About:

- Why it's important to choose a target accommodation
- Good target accommodations to reduce
- What makes an accommodation a poor choice to target
- Choosing your first target accommodation

9

Planning How to Reduce Accommodation

What Should Your Plan Include?

A good plan for reducing accommodation should be as detailed as possible. Take a look at these sample plans to get an idea of the kind of details your plan should have. Then read through the rest of the chapter, and you'll be ready to make your own plan, using Worksheet 8 (Your Plan) in Appendix A at the end of this book.

Sample Plan 1

Yazmin's plan was to reduce accommodation for her 12-year-old son Mohammad, whose anxiety caused him to be constantly worried about any possible change in the daily routines, and to want to know in advance exactly what was planned for each day. Yazmin had been providing accommodation by preparing a written schedule for each day and reviewing it with Mohammad each morning before school. The schedule was very detailed and included things like who was going to pick up Mohammad from school; the precise time Yazmin would be coming home from work if Mohammad got home first; whether Yazmin would be going out in the evening, and if so where she would go, the time she would leave, and the exact time she would get back. On weekends, the schedule included even more details of everything that Mohammad or Yazmin would be doing over the entire day. Yazmin felt that making the schedules was not only time-consuming to her, but also made her feel more anxious because she worried about Mohammad's reaction if there was any deviation from the schedule.

Yazmin's plan was:

1. *Mamma (Yazmin) will not write out any schedules.*
2. *Mamma will not discuss when she will get home from work, but will call Mohammad at home if she is going to get home later than the usual time of 6:15 P.M.*
3. *Mamma will not answer questions about her evening plans in the morning (or the day before) but will tell Mohammad at least an hour before going out.*
4. *If Mamma goes out in the evening, she will not answer questions about when she will come home, but will tell Mohammad if she expects to be home later than his bedtime (8:45 P.M.).*
5. *If Mamma originally did not expect to be out later than Mohammad's bedtime and is not going to be home by 8:45, Mamma will call Mohammad on the phone to say goodnight.*
6. *Mamma will tell Mohammad the weekend activities that he is going to be involved in, but will not write them on a schedule.*
7. *If Mohammad asks questions about the schedule, Mamma will reply one time with a supportive statement (I get that you worry about the schedule, but I'm sure you can handle the worry on your own). After the first question, Mamma will not reply again.*
8. *Every weekend will include at least one hour of unplanned time during which Mamma will suggest to Mohammad one activity that they had not planned (and Mohammad may choose not to participate).*

Notice the level of detail in Yazmin's plan. She has even thought about some of the likely questions that may come up in trying to implement her plan. For example, Yazmin realized that Mohammad is upset by sudden changes from routine and would find it hard if she were to go out in the evening without any advance warning. She does not want to commit to having to plan every evening in advance, and so she has decided that she will not discuss her evening plans in advance, but she will give Mohammad at least one hour of notice if she decides to go out. Yazmin also realized that sometimes changes to the schedule can happen unexpectedly. She does not want to discuss her work schedule with her son each morning, or to promise to be home at a certain time. Yazmin does agree, however, that Mohammad is entitled to know about changes to the routine, and so she has agreed to call him at home if she is staying late at work.

Notice also how all of the points on Yazmin's plan relate only to *her* behavior. There is nothing in her plan about what Mohammad will do. The reason, of course, is that Yazmin does not know, and cannot decide, what her child will do. He may accept the plan without difficulty, or he may continue to ask her for the usual schedules. He may call her at work to ask when she is getting home. He may even become angry or distressed at the change and react explosively. Yazmin cannot decide how Mohammad will act—but she doesn't have to! For her plan to be successful, she only needs to control her own behavior and have confidence that Mohammad will cope.

Take a look at the last point on Yazmin's plan. She has decided to introduce some unplanned time to help Mohammad become more accustomed to the idea of not knowing exactly what will happen at every stage of his day. But here, too, Yazmin is acknowledging that she can only control her own behavior. She is explicitly accepting that Mohammad may choose not to engage in the unscheduled activity. She will try to plan something fun, in the hopes that he will be motivated to participate and learn that unplanned things can still be fun. But her plan is entirely focused on her behavior (offering the activity), rather than on what Mohammad will or will not do.

Sample Plan 2

Ally and Frankie made a plan to reduce the accommodation they had been providing for their daughter, Aubree, who was 15 years old and suffered from recurring panic attacks. When she had a panic attack, Aubree would be engulfed in waves of anxiety, with racing heart, difficulty breathing, dizziness, and the strange sensation of feeling like her body was smaller than usual, or everything else had become extra large. The panic attacks were very frightening for Aubree, who had become reluctant to go places unaccompanied by her parents, and would use her Fitbit wristband to constantly check her heart rate throughout the day. If she noticed any elevation in heart rate, she would become very anxious, and her parents would accommodate by immediately reassuring her that she was OK and repeatedly checking her heart rate with her until she was convinced she was not having a panic attack. Because Aubree's anxiety about having a panic attack actually caused her heart rate to increase, her parents would often encourage her to lie down in bed, and would lie next to her, stroking her hair, helping her to breathe slowly, and speaking soothingly until the anxiety subsided.

Ally and Frankie decided to focus their first plan for reducing accommodation on the times when Aubree noticed her heart rate going up, rather than on the need to accompany her places. They were concerned that refusing to go places with their daughter would cause Aubree to stop going out altogether. They hoped that reducing their other accommodations first would help Aubree become less anxious, making it easier to tackle going places as a second target later on. Frankie and Ally's plan was:

1. *We won't check Aubree's heart rate or become involved in her checks.*
2. *We won't answer questions about Aubree's heart rate more than one time per day.*

3. *If Aubree asks us about her heart rate or about panic attacks, we will say, "Aubree, we understand that panic attacks are very uncomfortable and that you are really scared of having another one. We know that even if you have a panic attack, you will handle it and be OK in the end."*

4. *If Aubree repeatedly asks us questions about her anxiety, or requests that we check her heart rate with her, we will say the above one time, and then go into another room.*

5. *If Aubree asks us to lie down next to her when she is anxious, we will agree to spend up to five minutes helping her to breathe slowly. After five minutes, if Aubree is still anxious, we will say, "I see that you are still feeling pretty anxious, but I know it will pass and you will be OK. I'm going now." We will then leave Aubree alone and go to another room.*

6. *Neither of us will lie down next to Aubree to help her breathe more than two times on any given day.*

As you can see from their plan, Ally and Frankie had thought about the possibility that Aubree would continue to request their reassurance and accommodation even after they informed her of their plan. They realized that they could not count on Aubree stopping her requests for accommodation simply because they said they would not provide it. They knew they could only control their own behavior—not their daughter's! They also realized how hard it might be not to provide the accommodation when Aubree is feeling very anxious and repeatedly asking them for help. Their plan reflected this concern, and their solution was to remove themselves from the situation if not providing accommodation became too difficult for them. Going to another room and leaving Aubree alone when she is feeling anxious or panicky can seem like a harsh or uncaring act, but Frankie and Ally cared deeply about their daughter. They understood that being in the same room when Aubree was pleading with them for help would be incredibly hard, and they knew they might not succeed and could succumb to providing the accommodation.

Ally and Frankie had confidence that Aubree would be OK and would be able to tolerate the anxiety even if she actually had a panic attack. By leaving the room, the parents hoped they would be able to show Aubree how confident they were in her ability to cope with the anxiety. These parents also understood that staying near Aubree when she is anxious and asking for their help, might actually make the experience worse for Aubree. Having her parents right there next to her, but refusing to engage with her anxiety, could be extremely frustrating for the girl, and as long as her parents were beside her, Aubree might find it much harder to stop asking for accommodation. Having her parents leave the room may feel bad to Aubree at first, but once she realizes they are not around, Aubree would be more likely to find in herself the strength to cope with the fear.

This element of the plan, going to another room and leaving Aubree to cope alone, brings up an important point about childhood anxiety and family accommodation. Children who have come to rely on accommodation for help in coping with anxiety often will think of the accommodation as the only means of coping. As long as your child remains hopeful that you may provide the accommodation, they are much less likely to try out other ways of coping. Once your child sees that you are definitely not going to accommodate, she is more likely to find other, more independent means of regulating her own anxiety.

Ally and Frankie's strategy of lying on the bed and breathing with Aubree reflects this shift toward more independent coping. By breathing slowly and deeply, Aubree was using her body to regulate her anxiety. Rather than seeing this as a skill to use anytime she was feeling anxious, however, Aubree viewed the relaxing breathing as something that her parents did for her. The accommodation was turning an excellent coping strategy, one which could help Aubree become less vulnerable to her anxiety, into something that maintained her dependence on her parents. Frankie and Ally wanted to continue to encourage Aubree to use her breathing to help herself calm down, but they also wanted her to see the breathing as a tool of her own, something she could do independently to feel better. That is why the parents included two specific things in their plan:

1. They limited the amount of time they would spend with Aubree helping her to breathe. By imposing the 5-minute time limit, the parents made it likely that they would sometimes have to leave before Aubree had completely calmed down. This would allow Aubree to have opportunities to continue using the breathing on her own, after they had left.
2. They limited the number of times each day that they would do the breathing with their daughter. Limiting the number of times they would lie down next to her made it likely that sometimes Aubree would have to practice the breathing on her own if she wanted to use her body to lower her anxiety.

Finally, notice one more thing: Frankie and Ally made a specific plan for what they would say to Aubree when they implemented their plan not to accommodate. They had a plan for what to say when leaving the room rather than providing reassurance or checking her heart rate. Their plan allowed them to replace the accommodating behavior of staying with Aubree and reassuring her, with a supportive response. They also had a plan for what they would say if they reached the 5-minute time limit for helping her with relaxation and soothing. Having a specific plan that they could practice and role-play in advance, helped them to avoid having to improvise their responses in the moment and allowed them to be consistent. The plan helped them to be consistent both across the various situations and between themselves so that they would both say the same thing. Frankie and Ally were careful to choose supportive statements to make in those difficult moments. Both of the phrases they chose included the two ingredients of support: acceptance (*We understand that panic attacks are very scary and that you are really scared of having another one; I see that you are still feeling pretty anxious.*) and confidence (*We know that even if you have a panic attack, you can handle it and you will be OK in the end; I know it will pass and you will be OK.).*

Sample Plan 3

Lewis made a plan for reducing accommodation of his son Keagan's anxiety. Keagan was 11 years old and had suffered from obsessive-compulsive disorder (OCD) for several years. Most recently, his OCD centered on the fear that he had done something bad or that he would do something bad or even criminal in the future. Keagan would review his day very carefully before going to bed every night, and Lewis would sit with his son and listen to his detailed descriptions of everything that happened that day, reassuring the child that nothing he had done was bad or against the law. The nightly ritual would last for over half an hour, and sometimes much longer. Lewis would also reassure Keagan that there was no reason to suppose he would suddenly become a bad person or a criminal. Lewis would tell the child over and over that he was in control of his own behavior and that he had the choice to act well or not. Lewis would try to provide Keagan with statistics on the frequency of various crimes and the factors that predict whether someone will act badly. Lewis would even make up statistics about crime and criminality that he hoped would help Keagan stop worrying about his future behavior. Despite all of the father's efforts, however, Keagan never seemed reassured for more than that one night, and the next evening the entire process would repeat itself all over again, with Keagan asking the same questions and Lewis providing the reassuring answers.

Lewis's plan was:

1. *Dad will not review the day with Keagan.*
2. *If Keagan wants to tell Dad something about the day, Dad will listen but will stop listening or responding if he thinks Keagan is*

checking for bad behavior or seeking reassurance that he has not done something bad.

3. *Dad will not talk with Keagan about his day after suppertime.*

4. *Dad will not answer questions about whether Keagan will do something bad in the future.*

5. *If Keagan is asking for reassurance or wants to review the day, Dad will say one time, "Keagan, I love you, and I know the OCD is very hard on you because you have very unpleasant thoughts. I am sure you will be OK, and I don't think it helps for me to talk with you about this. My job is to help you, and I think I'm helping you more by not answering anymore." Dad will only say this one time, and after that will not answer or respond to Keagan's OCD requests.*

Like the other plans, Lewis is trying to be as detailed as possible. He understands that the process can be difficult and has made a plan for how to respond supportively instead of accommodating. Lewis also has to contend with another difficulty. He does not want to stop talking with Keagan altogether, and he still wants to show his son that he cares about the things that happen to him and takes an interest in his day. But Lewis wants to stop providing accommodation by reviewing Keagan's day in an OCD manner. His solution has two components:

1. Lewis plans to continue listening to Keagan and talking with him about his day, as long as Keagan is not drawing him into compulsive OCD checking and reassuring. Note that there is not one clear definition for when something Keagan says is simply talking about the day, and when it is an OCD behavior. There is no way for Lewis to list all the possible things Keagan might say to him and plan a response for each. Instead, Lewis plans that if he realizes during an interaction with Keagan that the conversation has become an OCD accommodation, he will stop engaging in the interaction. Of course, Keagan might not agree that he is doing OCD talk, and he may argue

that he just wants to share details of his day. The important thing is that Keagan does not have to agree for Lewis to be able to implement his plan. This is why ensuring that the accommodation plan is all about the parent's behavior, and not the child's, is so important. Lewis will rely on his own judgment and will act according to what he thinks is most correct in each situation, whether or not Keagan agrees. Is it possible that Lewis will get it wrong sometimes and think something is an OCD behavior when it isn't? Yes, this is a possibility. And, of course, the opposite can also occur. Lewis might think something is not an OCD behavior when it actually is, leading him to provide reassurance and accommodation. Lewis has probably gotten pretty good by now at recognizing OCD talk, but he could get it wrong sometimes. and that is OK. The worst that will happen is that Keagan will sometimes be frustrated because his father is not having a conversation with him, or will occasionally be accommodated despite the plan. That is unfortunate, but the alternative is to refrain from accommodation only when Keagan agrees that his behavior is OCD driven. Keagan is probably going to be very strongly motivated to get the accommodation from Lewis, and that could cause him to deny that he is experiencing an OCD worry even when he knows that he is. He also might not himself realize when a worry is related to his OCD. By exercising his own judgment and acting accordingly, Lewis is taking the burden of recognizing the OCD off of Keagan's shoulders and taking the responsibility himself.

2. The second element of Lewis's plan for coping with the difficulty of recognizing OCD talk while still remaining available to talk with Lewis about his life, is to limit conversations about the day to before suppertime. Lewis knows that the time between supper and bedtime is when Keagan is most likely to be worried by his OCD and to engage in his daily review and accommodation. So Lewis has decided that conversations about

the day have to happen before supper. Of course, Keagan could still seek accommodation before suppertime, and then Lewis will have to implement his plan not to respond. Also, Keagan could just want to share something about his day that occurs to him after supper, in which case, he will have to wait until the next day to talk about it with his dad. By stopping the conversations about the day at suppertime, Lewis is hoping to make the process of not accommodating easier.

No plan is perfect, and the plan you make to reduce the target accommodation you provide to your child with anxiety is not going to be perfect either. That is OK! The important thing is to think through the details of the plan as much as possible, consider which things will make it challenging to implement, and then move forward with putting it into practice. You may need to make adjustments to your plan when you encounter a difficulty you had not considered, and this is also to be expected. You'll simply make the necessary changes and keep working!

Making Your Own Plan

Now you are ready to make your own plan. Use Worksheet 8 (Your Plan) found in Appendix A at the end of this book, to craft your plan in as much detail as possible. Think through each of the following elements and write your plan on the worksheet:

What?

What is the accommodation you are planning to reduce or stop? Be specific about the behaviors you are going to change. Don't use general statements such as, "I won't accommodate" or "I won't provide reassurance." Instead, write out what you mean in detail using statements such as, "I won't answer questions about whether foods are healthy," or "I won't stay in the room once I've put my child in bed," or "I won't answer text messages about anxiety worries."

When?

Write down whether you will change the accommodation all the time or only during particular parts of the day. For example, if you have been driving a special route on the way to and from your child's school (as can happen when a child is anxious about being in a certain place, or near a particular store or building) and you plan to only make the change on the way back home from school, write that down. If you plan to make the change in both directions, write that instead. If the change will happen on certain days, or only on weekends, or only when both parents are home, or any other particular times, write it down clearly.

Also, think about whether the change in accommodation is only going to be in response to your child asking for accommodation, or whether it is something you will do on your own schedule, independent of your child's behavior. For example, if you have been accommodating by cooking special meals for your child, you may decide that you won't cook the special food anymore, and this would happen independently, not in response to your child's behavior. You will still need to plan for how to respond to your child at mealtime, but the change in accommodation could be occurring before your child is even involved. Likewise, if you have accommodated by coming home early from work, the change might be that you'll come home later on one or more days. This also would happen independently of what your child is saying or doing. On the other hand, if you have been accommodating by promising your child that you will stand near the door of the bathroom while he showers, the change would occur when he is showering and asking you to stay nearby.

Finally, write down when you will start implementing the plan. Is it right away? Are you planning to start work on your plan at a particular time, such as next weekend, or after an upcoming event such as your child's birthday party? Sometimes it makes sense to postpone implementing your plan for a little while. You might be waiting for your partner to return from a trip, for example, or you could be waiting for a change in your own schedule that will make implementing the plan easier. You probably don't want to delay too long, and you shouldn't be looking for excuses to put it off. But there can be situations where some brief delay makes sense. Other times the best course of action is to go ahead and start right away. Either way, note in your plan when you intend to start.

Who?

Does the plan involve only you, or is anyone else a part of it? If two parents are planning together and will both be implementing the same steps, note that on the worksheet. If the plan is somewhat different for each of you, write down how each will behave. If the plan involves someone else who is not a parent, for example, a friend or relative, make a note of that as well (and make sure that they know the plan and are in agreement!).

How and How Much?

Do you plan to limit the accommodation to a certain number of times per day or to a specific number of accommodations in each situation? Or do you plan to stop the accommodation altogether and to try your hardest not to do it at all? Any of these could be a good plan. Sometimes the first plan might be to limit the accommodation to only a few times, with the intent of further reducing or stopping the accommodation later on. Other times you might think it will be easiest to just stop the accommodation once and for all. Either way, write down your plan clearly with details about how much accommodation, if any, you are going to provide. That way you will always know how you are supposed to act. Try to avoid vague statements such as, "I will only answer *a few* questions each day." Vague statements will make it harder for you to decide whether or not to accommodate, and they will make it harder for your child to know what to expect. "A few" on one day might be different from "a few" on another day, making your behavior unpredictable and confusing for your child. Stating a clear number such as "only three questions each day," or "only for five minutes," will make your behavior much clearer and will make it easier for you to know whether you have already hit the limit of your plan.

You may be concerned that any number apart from zero will be confusing for your child. If you agree to provide the accommodation three times, won't that still make it hard for your child to know whether or not you are going to accommodate? The answer is no. In Chapter 10, you will learn some effective ways of communicating the plan to your child, so that she has a good understanding of exactly what you plan to change in your behavior. If you set a limit of three accommodations, then your child will know that, and she will understand that once the limit has been reached, you are no longer going to accommodate. A rule like that can be completely clear and consistent, as long as you make a detailed and specific plan.

What Will You Do Instead?

Think about how you will respond to your child when he is anxious and seeking accommodation. What will you do instead of accommodating? Are you going to offer some other suggestions? Will you remind him that you are working on not accommodating? Will you make a supportive statement to your child? Then what? Are you going to leave the room? Will you stay nearby and try to remain calm and composed? Is there anyone else who can help you to stick to the plan? Perhaps you plan to listen to some music to help you stay calm if your child is becoming distressed or angry with you for not accommodating? Even if your plan is as simple as, "I will just not respond," write that down on the accommodation plan worksheet.

Having a plan, any plan, is preferable to going into what may prove to be a difficult situation without a plan at all.

What Will Make This Hard?

Not every plan will to be easy to put into practice. Many things could make it hard for you to execute your plan consistently. Try to think about the challenges you are most likely to face. For example, if you plan to make a change to accommodations that occur before school, you may be concerned about getting your child to school on time and whether you will be able to stick with your plan if the morning drags on. Or, if you have other children, you might be concerned about how implementing your plan will affect them. You may wonder how much time this plan will take and whether you will be able to handle all the situations that can arise from it. Or you might be worried that your child will find some alternative to the accommodation that is also unhelpful or problematic. For example, if you have been accommodating by answering repeated phone calls at work, you may worry that if you do not answer, your child will call a coworker asking for you, causing them a disturbance. Thinking through these challenges in advance can help you to come up with solutions and not to be surprised. In the case of the phone calls, for example, you may want to explain to your coworkers that you are working with your child to overcome anxiety, and because you have made yourself less available, it is possible that they will hear from your child by phone.

Now that you've read through the tips and sample plans in this chapter, think carefully about your own plan and write it down on Worksheet 8. It might take you a few times to feel as though you've gotten it right, but it's worth putting in the effort. The more thought you put into your plan at this point, the easier it will be for you to communicate your plan to your child and put it into action. Once you've written down the plan, it's time to let your child know about it. Chapter 10 will cover how to inform your child about the plan in a supportive way. In the meantime, keep up the supportive statements and continue monitoring the target accommodation.

In This Chapter You Learned About:

- What your plan should include
- How to make your own plan for reducing your target accommodation
- Thinking through the challenges in implementing your plan

10

How Do You Let Your Child Know about the Plan?

Why Should You Tell Your Child about the Plan?

Now that your plan is ready, it's almost time to start reducing that accommodation! The last thing to do before putting your plan into action is to tell your child about it. Letting your child know what you plan to do is a good idea for a number of reasons, including that it is only fair to your child! You have been providing the accommodation, perhaps for a long time, and your child has no reason to expect that to change. She will be surprised and confused by the change in your behavior if you don't tell her about it beforehand. Explaining the plan in advance will also let her know that the change in accommodation is not a one-time thing. If you simply refuse to accommodate without explanation, your child might think that this is a temporary change, and she will likely expect you to accommodate the next time. Telling your child that this is now your regular plan and that you intend to always follow it, will prevent the misunderstanding.

Another reason to tell your child about the plan ahead of time is to give you an opportunity to explain why you are making the change. By now you will have been practicing making supportive statements as often as possible, and your child knows that you accept his anxiety, you don't judge it, and you have confidence he can cope with being anxious. If you haven't started saying this to your child, stop and practice making supportive statements for a few more days before continuing with your plan. The increase in supportive responses will prepare your child to understand the intent behind your plan, and describing the plan in advance will give you the chance to link the new plan to the same supportive approach.

In this chapter you will see how you can let your child know about the plan in a supportive way, expressing both acceptance and confidence. When you make this link, the plan itself becomes a powerful expression of support. Talking about the plan with your child allows you to explain that you are doing it precisely because you have confidence in her! Does this mean your child will be happy about the new plan? Of course it doesn't. But it does make it far more likely that she will understand that you have stopped accommodating because you believe in her and know she is strong enough to cope.

Describing the plan to your child will also help you to stay firm and committed to implementing it. If your child knows what you plan to do, you won't want to let him down. Remember, when you are reducing accommodation, you are not helping your child less—you are helping him more! If you tell your child that you are going to help him this way, it will be easier for you to stick with the plan if it turns out to be harder than you expect.

If you are wondering about whether your child is even aware of the accommodation, the answer is probably "yes." Research shows that most children are well aware of the accommodations their parents provide. In fact, in many cases children are even better at identifying accommodations than their parents. (You may do things because of your child's anxiety that you don't realize are accommodations!) Most children realize from their own experience that accommodation as a long-term strategy doesn't work. Of course, your child may want you to continue to accommodate because in the moment the accommodation can help her to feel better and less anxious. But over time she will have seen that despite all of your accommodations, she is still dealing with a lot of anxiety.

Your child might actually be able to help you improve the plan. Telling your child about the change you are going to make not only respects him as the person who is going to be directly affected by the change, but it also gives him an opportunity to offer feedback and input. For example, your child may point out challenges and obstacles that you hadn't thought of, and your plan could be improved by considering these challenges and planning solutions to them. Or perhaps your child suggests a slightly different change in accommodation. Telling your child about the plan is not the same as asking for his permission, but that doesn't mean he can't make a suggestion.

In the end, you are the one who will have to make the decision and carry out the plan, but taking your child's suggestions into consideration is a good idea. For example, if you planned to reduce accommodation by no longer staying with your child at her friend's house when you bring her over for a playdate, your child might suggest that you stay for 10 minutes before you leave. That seems like a reasonable starting step and one that you can definitely consider accepting. Your child is probably going to be less opposed to the plan, and the whole process may be much easier if she has had some input into the details. When you consider your child's suggestions seriously, it shows her that you are working to help her and that you respect her thoughts. But remember, the plan is still your plan! Even if your child makes a suggestion that you accept, she may still resist the actual implementation of the change. Don't expect your child to go along with the plan just because you told her about it in advance or took her suggestion.

Your plan is not a contract that you make with your child, and your child does not need to make any commitment to the plan. In fact, because the plan should be entirely about the changes in your own behavior, there should be no way for him to either comply with the plan or not. If in the end you think your child is "violating the plan," it is probably either because your plan includes details on what your child should be doing (rather than focusing only on what you will be doing), or because you are disappointed that he is not making it easier for you to carry out. If it is because the plan includes details on what your child will be doing, go back and revise your plan to focus only on what you will do. If you are disappointed that your child is still resisting the change in your behavior, just remember how hard this is on him, and accept that he is coping as best he can. Stay firm with your plan, and your child's response will soon improve.

When Should You Tell Your Child the Plan?

Don't wait until the last moment to tell your child about the changes you plan to make in the accommodation. When your child is anxious and expecting you to accommodate is not a good time to let her know that you have a plan, because her focus is going to be on becoming less anxious. She won't be able to think about much else, especially something that seems to be making things harder for her right now!

Choose a time when both you and your child are relatively calm. Even if this means postponing the start of the plan until the next day and providing accommodation one more time, it's worth it to give your child a chance to learn about the plan ahead of time and understand why you are doing it. If two parents are going to be involved in the plan, then try to find a time when you can tell your child about the plan together. You will have support from each other, and your child will know that you are both on the same page.

Pick a time when you can be free from other demands for at least a few minutes. Trying to tell your child about the plan at a busy time—while also answering e-mail, dressing a younger sibling, getting ready to walk out the door, or fielding phone calls—would be hard. Your child should also have a few minutes free to hear what you want to say. Some parents find that a car ride, on the way from an extracurricular activity, for example, is a good time to talk about the plan with their child. However, if you think your child is likely to become very upset and driving would be difficult, pick another time. You may even need to get a babysitter to look after your other children while you free up some time to talk with your highly anxious child. Having a babysitter while you're at home can seem silly, but knowing that there is someone else around who can respond to your other children's needs will make it easier for you to focus on the anxious child. Freeing yourself from other tasks and responsibilities, even for a short time, shows your child how important this is to you. If you make an effort to focus just on your child with anxiety, she will know it, and she will know this must be something important that you want to share.

What Should You Say?

The message you give your child to let him know about your plan for reducing accommodation has a few simple goals. It should let your child know *why* you are planning to reduce the accommodation, and it should let him know the *what, when, who,* and *how and how much,* of your plan. The *why* is the explanation for why you are going to be making a change. Make a supportive statement that clearly acknowledges that you know your child is anxious, worried, stressed, or afraid, and that you understand this is hard, but you know he is able to cope with feeling this way some of the time. Tell your child you realize that by providing the accommodation, you have not been helping him to get less anxious, and that you have decided to make a change to help him to get better. Framing the message in this way makes it clear that (1) your plan is intended to help him and (2) that you are taking responsibility for having provided the accommodation in the past. You're not blaming your child for requesting or relying on accommodation; you are simply acknowledging the truth that accommodation doesn't help, and you are shouldering the parental responsibility of doing what is best for your child.

The *what, when, who,* and *how* and *how much,* are the plan itself:

- **What:** Specific statement telling your child which accommodation or accommodations you intend to change.
- **When:** Tell your child when and in what situations you will be implementing your plan.
- **Who:** Tell the child who is going to be making the change.
- **How and How Much:** Be specific about the change in your behavior. What exactly are you going to do differently? How will you be responding now to the child's anxiety?

Be as clear and specific as possible. You can show your child the plan you wrote down on Worksheet 8 (Your Plan), and even give her a copy of her own to keep. Make sure that your child knows which accommodation you plan to reduce, how your behavior is going to change, and what you intend to do instead of accommodating. If you are working through this book together with a partner and they also will be making a change to their behavior, tell your child what each of you will be doing differently from what you were doing in the past.

Try to keep it brief! Don't make a long speech, and don't lecture your child about anxiety or coping. If you tend to ramble, practice saying just the *why* and the *what* and leave it at that. Your child has probably heard many admonishments and lectures from you in the past, and he might not want to hear another. Stay focused on the message, and leave anything else for another time. In particular, don't mix in other issues that you have been hankering to raise with your child. For example, if in addition to being anxious and relying on accommodation, your child is also not polite or respectful enough in your opinion, or if he doesn't put enough effort into his homework, or if you think he should do a better job at some other aspect of his life, leave all of that out of presenting your plan to reduce accommodation! Telling your child that you wish he was a better student probably won't help anyway (it rarely does), and it will only make the accommodation plan seem like just another area where you are dissatisfied with him.

Express confidence in your child's ability to cope, but apart from that and a brief positive statement you could include at the beginning, don't make other comments about your child's character or personality. You're not making this plan because your child is sullen or charming, quarrelsome or agreeable, lazy or diligent, friendly or standoffish, responsible or untrustworthy. You are making it simply because she is anxious and this is how you are going to help her. Children with anxiety come in all shapes and sizes, with every kind of personality. They do not have much in common apart from the fact that they are almost always accommodated by their parents. If your child was highly anxious but had a different personality, you would still be providing accommodation because that is how child anxiety works. Making the explanation about your child's personality is inaccurate and unfair, and is likely to antagonize her unnecessarily because it implies that the accommodation is somehow her fault, rather than a typical reaction on your part to your child being anxious.

In Appendix A at the end of this book, you will find Worksheet 9 (Announcement), which you can use to write your own message to your child with all the key elements. But first, here are sample messages from other parents, telling a child about the plan to reduce accommodation. First, you'll see two examples of messages that are not quite right. Try to think about what these parents could have done differently, and read the explanations following each. Then you'll see two examples of messages that do a better job of being brief, supportive, and specific.

Sample Message 1: What's Wrong with this Message?

Damien, we think you are a strong boy, and we have decided to help you to show it. We know that talking in school can be uncomfortable for you and we get that. But we also know that it's important for

you to be able to talk in school, with your friends and your teachers.
In the past we have asked your teachers not to call on you in class,
so as not to make you uncomfortable or embarrass you in front
of your friends. Now we think it is time for you to start showing
everyone how smart you can be, and we are no longer going to ask
your teachers not to call on you in class. It might be hard for you at
first, but you'll get used to it and start talking soon. We love to hear
you, and we know everyone else will as well! So proud of you, Dad
and Mom.

What do you think about this message from Damien's parents? Do you see anything they could have done better? Take a moment to read it over carefully while keeping in your mind the key elements of a good message to let a child know about the plan for reducing accommodation. The key elements are: a *supportive statement* about the child's anxiety problem and the reason *why* there is going to be a change in accommodation, followed by the *what, when, who,* and *how and how much* of the plan.

Let's see if Damien's parents had each of the elements of a good message:

Supportive Statement

By now you know that to be supportive, Damien's parents have to express acceptance and confidence. They do tell him that they know talking in school makes him uncomfortable (*acceptance*), but the second part of the statement seems a bit off. Instead of telling Damien they have confidence in his ability to tolerate the discomfort, they focus on how important it is that he begin to talk in school. This might seem to them like the same thing, but it probably doesn't feel like that to Damien. He is hearing them say that they know it's hard, but he has to do it anyway. That's very different from hearing them say that they know it's hard, but they believe in his ability to cope. Focusing on him doing it also has another disadvantage, compared with expressing confidence in his coping capacity. It shifts the focus away from the parents' behavior and on to Damien's. Now it seems as if the parents' message is going to be about their expectations of him, rather than about their intention to change an accommodation. Toward the end of their message, the parents do tell Damien that they believe he will get used to talking in school, which does seem to express confidence in him, but then they immediately add, "and start talking soon," putting the focus right back on his behavior rather than theirs.

Why

The parents have provided a reason for their behavior (for reducing this accommodation), but that reason is not about helping Damien to be less anxious, to cope better, or overcome his anxiety. Instead, Damien's parents have told him that they are making a plan so that he can start showing everyone how smart he is. That's a very different thing, and not necessarily a goal with which Damien identifies. It also implies that because he has not been speaking, people don't think Damien is smart right now, which may make him feel badly or raise a worry that he didn't have before. Remember to keep the focus on the anxiety and the accommodation, and stay away from other goals and traits.

What

Have Damien's parents clearly told him what accommodation they intend to change? They do mention one thing specifically: asking his teachers not to call on him in class. However, it is not entirely clear from their message what this means. Are they planning to actively ask his teachers to call on him, or will they simply stop asking teachers to refrain from calling on him? Presumably, Damien's parents don't speak with his teachers every day, making it hard to understand exactly what accommodation will change.

When

The message does not make clear when the parents' plan will be enacted and when the changes will impact him. Will Damien be called on every day? Every class? Only some of the time? When will it start? Including these details is what makes the plan a plan rather than a big-picture goal.

Who

Here it does seem clear that both parents are involved in the plan, and both are planning to make the same changes. If the plan is to actually start calling on him in class, then it would be helpful for Damien to know who, apart from his parents, is involved. Will it be all his teachers, or only some of them? Every class or some of his classes? The more details you provide your child about the plan, the easier it will be for him to predict what is going to happen and to understand it when it does.

How and How Much

Damien's parents have not given him much detail about how they are going to reduce the accommodation. As we've already noted under *who, when* and *what*, the message is actually pretty vague. A detailed plan will include a lot more information on the specifics of the changes that will happen. When you make your plan for your child, try to be as clear and specific as possible. Ask yourself what questions your child might have and what questions you would have if you were hearing about this plan from someone else. Try to provide the answers ahead of time. Remember that this is going to be hard for your child. You are making a change in an area of his life that causes him a lot of stress and anxiety. The more details you provide, the easier it will be for him to come to terms quickly with the change. Seeing that you have put thought and effort into coming up

with a detailed plan also can increase your child's confidence that
you know what you're doing!

Sample Message 2: How Does this Message Fall Short?

*Paula, you have no idea how much you mean to us and how deeply
we care about you. We have always tried to do everything we can for
you, and to give you the best life you can possibly have. If we have not
always done right, or have made mistakes along the way, we're sorry.
We're only human and everybody makes mistakes—even parents.*

*When you started to develop OCD we were so worried for you.
As you may know, your aunt and grandmother also have struggled
with OCD, and we know it has been a huge challenge for them. We
want your life to be easier than theirs, and so we are always looking
for more ways to help you and are willing to do anything in the world
that can help. Like your aunt Clara, you also worry about germs and
dirt. This is a very common symptom of OCD and might even run
in the family. We have read many books and articles about OCD
and have learned some important information that we want to share
with you. There is something called "family accommodation," and it
almost always happens when a child has OCD. It means that parents
are going along with the OCD and helping their child to do rituals.
It turns out that family accommodation is a bad thing. We have
been doing a lot of family accommodation ourselves. We wash our
hands whenever you ask, buy you a lot of extra soap because you are
always running out, give you all those little bottles of Purell that you
go through almost every week, and change our clothes whenever you
ask us to because you think we might have touched something dirty.
These are all family accommodations.*

*Now that we know that family accommodation is not a good
thing, we are going to try to stop doing it. So no more extra soap
and Purell, and no more hand washing. No more accommodation!
Whenever you think we are doing family accommodation, you*

should tell us so that we can stop. We're not perfect and we are
probably going to make lots of mistakes, but this is our plan and we
are doing it because nothing is more important to us in the whole
world than our little girl. Please believe that we only have your best
interests at heart and want you to live a wonderful and beautiful life
like you deserve. Your (not perfect), Mom and Dad.

What do you think about the message Paula's parents have given her? It is certainly from the heart! It would be impossible to miss the love that they feel for her, and it is remarkably open and honest, reflecting an outpouring of emotions, including love, concern, guilt, and the desire to be understood. Being open and honest with your child is a good thing, but does this message actually do what it is intended to do? Does it fill its primary purpose of letting Paula know about the changes her parents are planning to make in a clear and supportive way? What do you think Paula feels when she gets this message from her parents? She may feel some guilt of her own, at her parents clear distress brought on by her OCD. She may feel scared at the comparisons to her aunt and grandmother for whom the OCD has been "a huge challenge" all their lives. She may feel badly about causing this thing called "family accommodation," which she is hearing is "bad." Paula may feel bewildered by her parents apologies for mistakes they tell her they have made in raising her, or she may want to reassure them that she knows they are doing their best and that they are good parents. She may be confused about what exactly her parents are asking of her when they encourage her to tell them not to accommodate. Those are a lot of feelings, and some are quite hard for a child to be saddled with. By the time her parents finish their lengthy introduction, Paula may be too confused or overwhelmed to even focus on what they are trying to tell her about their plan.

Now think about the things that Paula is not hearing in her parents' message. She is not hearing a clear expression of confidence in her ability to cope with the distress of obsessive thoughts and compulsive urges. Without an expression of confidence, a message can be accepting, but it cannot be supportive. Paula's parents have also not explained the rationale for what they intend to do, the *why*. They have told her that accommodation is a bad thing but not why it is bad, or how their plan is better. Bad is a strong word with a lot of emotional charge, but it is not an explanation. It is hard to guess how Paula understands the word bad—whether as a moral thing or a practical one—and it would be better if there was no need to guess. If her parents explained to her that accommodation is unhelpful in overcoming OCD, or that it can maintain the symptoms of OCD, and that they will try to accommodate less so that she can get better, the *why* would be much clearer.

Paula is also not hearing a clear *what, when, who,* and *how and how much*. In fact, she is not actually hearing a plan at all! It is clear that her parents mean to accommodate less, but that is a goal (and a rather vague one) rather than a plan. The *what* part of the message should clearly let Paula know which accommodations are the focus of the plan. Her parents have described a number of accommodations (buying extra soap, providing many bottles of Purell, washing their hands, and changing their clothes). Any one of these accommodations would make a good target for the plan, but they have not told her which the target is. They say, "No more extra soap and Purell, and no more hand washing." This is a lot of accommodation for one plan, and more than they should probably be taking on at one time. But they also add, "No more accommodation!" making it sound like the plan actually applies to all accommodation all the time.

The *when, who,* and *how and how much* parts of the message should translate the goal of reducing specific accommodations into concrete changes that the parents are going to make, with as much detail as possible. Paula's parents have not given her any information about the specific steps or changes they are going to make. Will they never wash their hands at all? Will there be no more Purell, or only some? And if there will be some, then how much? What will they do when the soap runs out? And, of course, there can be no specific plan for the other unspecified accommodations that they are also suggesting they are going to stop. Clearly the parents have spoken from the heart, but the strong feelings they have about their daughter's OCD have gotten in the way of formulating a simple and clear message that would be useful to Paula and would help the whole family to adjust to the process of providing less accommodation.

When you think of the message that you want to give your child to let her know about your plan for reducing accommodation, try to keep it simple. If you have strong feelings of guilt, sadness, or worry for your child because she is anxious, that is completely natural, and this means you care deeply about your child. But try to keep those feelings separate from the message about your plan. Say out loud, or write down and read to yourself, what you intend to say, and ask yourself whether your message is brief, supportive, clear, and specific. Anything that is getting in the way of that is not helping.

Sample Message 3: Example of a Good Message

Elle, we love you very much and think you are a wonderful child. We know you've been very worried about choking ever since you had that incident at the restaurant. That was really scary for all of us, and we know how frightening it is for you to think about choking again. We also know that you are a strong person, and that you can be OK even with feeling scared sometimes. We've been cutting your food for you into very small pieces ever since that day, but we've realized that by doing this, we've not actually been helping you to overcome this fear. Now that we understand this, we've decided to make a change, so that we can help you better. From now on Mom and Dad are not going to cut your food anymore. We also won't be answering questions about whether a food is dangerous or will make you choke. If you ask us, we'll remind you of this plan one time. After that, we won't talk about it anymore. We know this will be hard for you at

*first, but we have 100% confidence in you! We love you and we're
sure you'll be feeling much less scared soon.*

Notice in this message that the parents have acknowledged how le-
gitimate their daughter's fear is. Elle and her parents had had quite a
fright when the girl experienced choking at a restaurant. Sometimes
a stressful event such as choking will cause the onset of severe anxiety in a child, particularly if that child was already predisposed to
elevated fear or anxiety levels.

Elle's parents have managed to make a supportive statement at the
beginning of their message. They accept that Elle is afraid and they
don't blame her! They have combined the message of acceptance
with one of confidence in their child. (Remember the formula: acceptance + confidence = support.) They've also taken responsibility
for having accommodated Elle so far, and they have expressed their
determination to help her by accommodating less in the future. There
is no blame placed on Elle, and it is clear that this statement is all
about what the parents plan to do, not what they expect of their child.

After a supportive and brief opening to their message that gives
Elle the *why* for what they are doing, the parents follow up with a
clear description of the accommodations they mean to reduce (the
what) and provide details about the *when* (at mealtimes; the implied rule is that this applies to all mealtimes, although the parents
could have been more specific about that), *who* (both parents), and
the *how and how much* (they will no longer cut her food or answer
questions about choking and food safety). They have also told Elle
what they intend to do instead (respond only once with a supportive
reminder of the plan, and then not discuss it any further).

Finally, Elle's parents ended the message with another statement of support and hope. They express their love for her and
they're done!

Delivering this message probably didn't take Elle's parents more
than one minute. It really doesn't take any longer if you keep it short,
clear, and to the point.

Sample Message 4: Another Good, Complete Message

Jaxon, I'm very proud of you, you're a wonderful kid! Recently I've seen how worried you are about getting anywhere late, especially school. I know this is a real worry and that you try hard not to be late, but I also know that you are strong enough to handle worries. I thought that I was helping you by waking you up so early in the morning and agreeing to leave for school half an hour early. Now I know that doing these things is actually the wrong way to help. I've learned more about how to help you, and from now on I am going to do things differently. I will go back to waking you at the usual time like I always did (6:30), and instead of leaving for school half an hour early at 7:10, I will only agree to leave the house 10 minutes early, at 7:30. Even if we are ready before 7:30, I won't leave until then. I know that I've gotten upset with you some days, and I am sorry for that, but I want you to know that I am not making these changes to punish you or because I'm mad. The worry is not your fault at all. I am making the changes to help you get better and be less worried. It might be tough for both of us at first, but I'm sure it is the right thing to do, and I want to help you as best I can. You're going to be OK, and I think we'll both feel better soon!

P.S. On the mornings when you're at Dad's house, he is in charge and he will decide when to wake you and when to leave. Dad knows about my plan and understands why I am doing it.

What do you think about this message? Is it supportive, clear, and specific? Let's check. Using the formula of acceptance and confidence, we see that Jaxon's mother, Linda, has succeeded in expressing support. She tells Jaxon that she accepts his worry and how hard it can be, and she also lets him know that she has confidence in his ability to cope with worry. She's given him a clear *why* by letting him know she is making the change to help him feel better and because she believes this is the right way to do it. She avoided placing blame on Jaxon or including any demands for changes in the boy's behavior.

What about the *what, when, who,* and *how and how much?* It looks like Linda has provided clear answers to all of these questions. She lets her son know that the accommodations she's changing are waking him early and leaving early for school (*what*); she has made it clear that the plan applies only to the mornings when Jaxon is at her house and that Jaxon's father may choose to act differently, and that the plan goes into effect "from now on" (*when; who*); and she details the specific changes she is going to make for both forms of accommodation (*how and how much*).

Two additional things are worth noting about this message and plan. First, Linda has chosen to completely stop the accommodation of waking up Jaxon extra early, but she has decided to only partially reduce the accommodation of leaving the house early. Stopping an accommodation completely and reducing an accommodation partially are both good ways to help Jaxon to become less anxious. It may be that after implementing her plan for a while, Linda will decide to take it a step further and not leave the house early. In that case, she will simply make another supportive message and explain the new plan to Jaxon so that he understands and is prepared. It could also be that this next step proves unnecessary, whether because Linda decides that leaving at 7:30 is a reasonable strategy and no longer thinks it is an accommodation, or because Jaxon becomes less worried as a result of these changes and is no longer as preoccupied with being late and leaving early. Either way, starting with a partial accommodation can be a good plan, and the most important thing is that you have a plan, explain it clearly, and get to work.

Will Linda's plan be effective if Jaxon's father does not follow it? Will reducing her accommodation matter if Dad continues to accommodate at his house? The answer is yes! Reducing the accommodation consistently in the situations that you can control can work well even if there are other situations where the accommodation continues outside of your control. Jaxon will see that his mother has complete confidence in his ability to cope, and he will find that he is able to be OK in the mornings even without accommodation. His anxiety will probably go down even if his father disagrees with the plan or is not focused on the same thing. Remember that in this method you focus only on changing the things that you can actually control—not trying to force change on anyone else. You know that you can't control your child's thoughts, feelings, or behavior directly, and you will change your own behavior instead of causing unhelpful conflict by trying. And the same thing goes for all the other people in the world. You can't actually control any of them, and trying to force other people to change in accordance with your opinion, even if your opinion is correct, is more likely to result in conflict than to bring about the change you want. Of course, Jaxon's mother can try to explain to Jaxon's father what she has learned and see whether he is willing to make a plan together on which they can both agree. But if not, then she is wise to focus on the mornings at her own house.

Telling Jaxon in advance that the plan only applies to the mornings at her house is smart. This way the plan can be completely consistent, even if the father does not follow it. Consistency for Jaxon's plan means that his mother wakes him up at the normal time and does not leave for school more than 10 minutes early. If his father does otherwise, the plan is still entirely consistent, because those mornings were explicitly not part of the plan. This is why making the *when* and *who* parts of the plan very clear is smart. It allows Linda to turn something that may not be consistent into something that is! Once you think about it like that, you can realize that there are many things that are *consistent* without being *unchanging* because consistent and unchanging are two different things. For example, Jaxon probably goes to school consistently every school day, but he doesn't go to school on the weekends and holidays. Does this mean that his school schedule is inconsistent, unpredictable, or confusing? Of course not. Jaxon knows that if it's a school day there is school, and if it's a weekend there is not. It's entirely predictable and the rule is consistent. If Jaxon woke up every morning not knowing if there was going to be school because school days had somehow become random, that would definitely be confusing. But a schedule that varies according to a clear and explicit rule can still be a consistent schedule.

Using a Written Message

Now you're ready to use Worksheet 9 (Announcement), in Appendix A at the end of this book, to write down your own message to your child informing her about your plan for reducing accommodation. Once you've written it down, read it out loud to yourself (consider reading it to another person as well) to see how it sounds. Does it sound clear and supportive? If you think it's not quite right, make some changes (you can make copies of the worksheet or, if you prefer, type it on a computer) until you are confident about the message. Reading it out loud once or twice will also help it feel more natural when you deliver the message to your child.

When you think the message is ready, I strongly encourage you to make another copy that you will be able to read and give to your child to keep. Reading a written message and giving it to your child, has some very distinct advantages and is preferable to just telling the message to your child. The most important advantage is that reading your message out loud from a written text will help you to say exactly what you intend. When you are speaking, rather than reading, it's difficult to know what you're going to say. You may become confused or not remember exactly what you wrote on the worksheet. Or your child may distract you by interrupting or asking a question, causing you to change the wording to something different. If the brief, clear, and specific style of the message is not your usual style, you may find that you go back to your more typical way of talking. You have put a lot of thought into this message, and it would be wasted if you end up saying something else.

Using a written message can also help you to cope with the possibility that your child does not want to hear what you have to say. If he is not willing to listen, it will be easier to say the message anyway if you just read it from a paper and leave, than if you have to sit there and talk with a child who is not paying attention. If you have difficulty communicating with your child, or if your relationship is particularly strained and tense, then reading a written announcement is even more important and far superior to trying for a regular conversation and hoping it will go well. Remember this is not really a conversation; rather, it is a message from you to your child. Your child may have input and reactions, and that is OK, but the important thing is the information you want to give to him. Reading the message is less likely to turn into a debate or argument, than trying to talk with him as usual.

The written message is also something you can give to your child, which she can read over again later if she chooses. Even a child too young to read may want to keep your written message and can appreciate receiving it. Your child might have a hard time focusing on the things you want her to hear because she is anxious or upset. If you give her a copy of the message, she can always read it over when she's feeling calmer. Of course, your child might choose not to read the message, and that is OK, too. Even if she throws it away to show you that she doesn't like it or because it makes her feel upset, it's not a problem. You are there to let her know your plan and why you are doing it, and your child is free to respond with whatever response feels right to her in that moment.

It may feel odd or strange to you to be reading a written message to your child! It does seem a bit more formal than most conversations between parents and children, but that is all right. In fact, it is a good thing for the situation to feel a little unusual or different. This will let your child know that it *is* different. He will see that you are really thinking about things and starting something that is different from things you've done in the past. The formality can give the situation a sense of importance and even excitement that will make it feel special. Children react in all different ways to written announcements, and it is not unusual for them to feel very important because their

parents have taken the time to think about how to help them and
have written down a plan that is just for them.

Challenges in Telling Your Child the Plan

You're ready to share the plan with your child:

- You've thought about how you are going to inform your child
  about your plan to reduce accommodation.
- You've made sure that your message is brief and clear and
  includes a *supportive statement* and the *why, what, when, who,*
  and *how and how much* of your plan.
- You've chosen a good time when both you and your child are
  free to focus on what you have to say.
- Now you're ready to let your child know what you have
  in mind.

Delivering your message to your child could still turn out to be difficult, and it is good to be prepared for some of the more common
difficulties. As you read through this section, think about which
challenges are most likely to apply to you and your child, and consider the advice for how to handle them. But don't worry if things
don't turn out quite as you expect. The important thing is that you've
done your best to prepare your child for your next steps and . . . you
can't control what he does!

Your Child Doesn't Want to Hear It

You may find that your child is not interested in hearing what you
have to say. This can be frustrating and disappointing, especially because you've put a lot of effort into crafting such a careful and supportive message. But don't be surprised if your child is not keen on

hearing it. Perhaps he is thinking that you are going to repeat things you've already said, and he doesn't want to hear them again. If you previously focused on the changes you expect in your child, or on things you said that sounded as though you were blaming him for the anxiety, he may be particularly reluctant to hear this new message.

Or perhaps talking about his anxiety makes your child uncomfortable, or brings up the anxious feelings. It may be that he is worried that you are planning changes he won't like. It may be that his lack of interest has little to do with the content of your message—for example, he may be feeling bad or upset with you for reasons not related to the anxiety. He may want to do something else or talk about something else at that moment.

Whatever the reason, it is not worth getting into a heated argument. Even if you were to win the argument and capture your child's attention, it is unlikely that he would be open to hearing and thinking about what you have to say, if he feels as though he is listening against his will. Try to make it clear that (1) you have a short thing to say, (2) it will just take a minute, and (3) it is something new. Let your child know that he is not required to answer or do anything special, and that you've put a lot of thought into what you want to tell him. If he is still not interested in hearing it, don't push it. You can simply say your piece and go. Or if you feel as though you are unable to talk to him at all, consider giving him the written message instead. Even if he doesn't read it, you'll be able start putting your plan into action, and if your child is confused by your actions, you can offer to read him the announcement at that point and give him another copy.

Your Child Becomes Anxious or Upset

If you see that your child is becoming very upset at the content of your message, your instinct might be to stop and comfort her. It's natural to want your child to feel better and not to want to say something that is causing her distress. But try to wait until you have finished telling her the plan before you attempt to console her. That way your child will know that even though you understand it is hard, you are still determined to help her. It won't take long to get through your plan, and you'll have time to soothe her after she knows what you intend to do.

Stopping the message because your child is upset has two disadvantages in addition to preventing you from giving her the information she needs:

1. It teaches your child that if she is upset, you can't follow your plan. This is not a good lesson because it will probably mean that your child will work hard to show you how upset she is when you actually are reducing the accommodation. It is important that your child understands that even though you care deeply about her feelings, you sometimes have to do the thing you believe is best—even if that makes her uncomfortable.

2. It also conveys something very different from support. To be supportive, you show your child that you have confidence in her ability to tolerate distress. If you stop the message because of her distress, this is an indication that you don't actually think she can tolerate it. Otherwise why would you stop?

So take a deep breath, finish saying what you meant to say, and then if your child is still upset, you can try to help her feel better. Accept that it might take her a little while to calm down, but remain confident that in the end, she will.

Your Child Becomes Angry

If your child becomes angry at you for letting him know that you intend to reduce the accommodation, don't be surprised! Why wouldn't he be angry? You're telling him that you are planning to take away something he relies on a lot. Wouldn't you be angry if someone took away from you, without your permission, something you know is very important to you, and which you rely on to cope with a big problem in your life? Of course you might get mad at them. The important thing is not to get angry back. If you remind yourself how natural it is for your child to respond with some anger to your plan, it will be easier for you to see his anger as a natural expression of his anxiety, and to be empathetic rather than hostile.

Remember back in Chapter 1, where I discussed the concept of fight or flight, which describes the physical systems that ramp up when we are anxious? When people are scared, their bodies prepare to deal with the threat by activating this system. During fight or flight, our blood pressure goes up, our heart rate increases, our breathing becomes more rapid, and our emotions change.

Most people associate the fight or flight response with the emotion of fear. We feel afraid and that helps us to run away as fast as possible, using the boost of energy our bodies produce. But fear and running away are only half of the response. Running away is "flight," but what about "fight"? When this system of acute stress response is triggered, it can just as easily make us fight as run away, and the emotions that drive us to fight include not just fear, but also anger and even rage. Your child's anger can be just as powerful an indication of his anxiety as is his fear, so remind yourself of the fight part of fight or flight if your child becomes angry at you when you tell him about your plan. Tell yourself, "This is just my child's anxiety; I don't blame him for being upset." Then take a deep breath, stay calm, and stay on message.

Even if you think your child's response is inappropriate or disrespectful and that it is your job to set boundaries on his behavior, this is not the time to teach your child a lesson. If you let his anger distract you from talking about your plan and shift your focus to his unacceptable behavior, then the anxiety will have succeeded in creating avoidance. You may think you are disciplining your child, but you probably are helping him to avoid something that makes him anxious. Have confidence that your child can tolerate hearing your plan. Once things calm down, if you still feel the need to address his actions, you can do so then, when both of you are calm and the message about the accommodation has been delivered.

Your Child Argues with You

Your child may try to change your mind about the plan. Why wouldn't she? If she doesn't like the plan, why not try to talk you out of it? You can listen to what your child has to say and consider useful suggestions if she makes any, but don't get into an argument. Arguments happen when two people want to change each other's minds. If your child wants to change your mind, it makes sense for her to engage you in an argument. But you don't have to change your child's mind at all. If you remember that it is neither possible nor necessary to make your child agree with the plan, it will be easy for you to stay out of the argument. Once you accept that your child doesn't have to agree and that you can still act in the way you believe is best, stopping the argument will be easy. Your child may continue to argue, but there is no need for you to argue back. Just tell her one time that this is what you think is best and this is what you are going to do, and then let it be. When your child sees that you are not participating in the argument, it will get easier for her to stop.

Here's a little trick you can use to help you stay out of an argument with your child. (This works for other arguments too—not just those about anxiety and accommodation.) Imagine that your child is trying to play ping-pong with you, but you don't want to play. Your child picks up the ball and hits it toward you. You don't want to play so you throw the ball back and say, "I'm not playing." Your child hits it to you again, and you pick it up, maybe a little angrily now, and throw it right back to her. Your child hits it to you once more and again you throw it back. Do you see what is happening? You don't want to play, so you keep throwing the ball back. But as long as you keep throwing it back, your child is just going to hit to you again. You're saying you don't want to play ping-pong, but that's exactly what you're doing. It's as if by trying not to play you actually *are* playing. If you really don't want to play, what can you do? The best thing is to ignore the ball completely. Let it bounce off of you and roll to the floor. Your child might pick it up and hit it to you again, but if you keep letting it bounce and roll, she is not going to keep it up forever. The ball is like your child's arguments, when you don't want to argue. If you keep throwing the argument back to her, she probably won't stop. Tell yourself, "I'm not playing. I'm just going to let it bounce and roll," and you'll see how much faster the arguments stop.

There's another good reason not to argue back if your child is persuading you to back off from your plan. If you continue to argue, you are probably giving your child the feeling that there is a chance that you can be persuaded. Just the fact that you continue to discuss it will make her think there is a chance she will win the argument. It may surprise you, but when a parent continues to discuss an issue, even if what they are saying is consistently the same, children usually take it to mean that the answer might change. If you are puzzled by this consider the following scenario:

> *Your child comes home from school one day and asks you to buy him a fifty-thousand-dollar Rolex watch. Of course (I assume), you're not going to buy him a watch like that, so you say, "Of course not!" but he continues to ask for the Rolex. Are you going to argue with him about it? Probably not. You know you're never going to buy it and that it's a waste of time to talk about it. You probably tell him very clearly that it's not happening, and if he continues to ask, you'll probably just ignore it because the discussion is silly. Most children know their parents well, and they know that if you are still having the discussion, it means you're not one hundred percent sure of your answer, even if you say you are. So they're going to keep at it. If you continue to argue with your child about your plan, you're not only giving him the impression that you won't be able to follow the plan unless you get him to agree (which is not correct), you're also letting him know that if he keeps arguing long enough and thinks of the right thing to say, there's a chance you'll change your mind.*

If your child thinks this, then the chances he'll stop the argument on his own are slim.

You've Told Your Child the Plan, So What Happens Next?

Once you've delivered your message, it's time to start putting your plan into action. From now on, your mission is to stick to your plan as consistently as you can. The more consistent you are in implementing your accommodation plan, the sooner you will see your child's anxiety going down. You may not always succeed, but keep on trying. Research shows that parents who consistently increase their supportive responses to their child's anxiety and decrease the accommodations they provide, are as effective at reducing their child's anxiety as individual cognitive behavioral therapy delivered directly to the child. The next chapter is all about implementing your plan and by now you're ready to do just that!

In This Chapter You Learned About:

- Why you should tell your child about the plan
- When you should tell your child about the plan
- Making sure your message is brief and supportive and includes the *why, what, when, who,* and *how and how much* of your plan
- Why you should use a written message
- What happens next

11

Working on Your Plan

Keep a Log

Now that you are beginning to put into practice your plan to reduce accommodation, it will be important to keep track of the times you were able to follow the plan as you intended, the times when you needed to make some change to the plan, and the times when you either forgot or something made it not possible to follow the plan. Use Worksheet 10 (Monitoring Target Accommodation) in Appendix A at the end of this book, to keep a log and monitor your progress. Writing down how it goes and what difficulties you encounter will help you to figure out the challenges, troubleshoot and plan solutions, and identify changes that might be needed to make the plan more feasible. Write down as many situations as possible using just enough words to help you understand later what happened. For example, if your child feels anxious when the TV is not set to a specific volume and your plan involves setting it to a different level, you might quickly jot down, "Tuesday PM. Parents visiting, didn't want a fight in front of them. Set to old level." Or if your plan is not to speak in place of your child with social anxiety, you could log, "Dinner at Francesco's. Didn't order for M. She didn't get anything, shared R's food."

What to Expect at First

The first time you implement your plan not to provide accommodation can be hard! Be prepared for the possibility that your child will become anxious, upset, or angry. Remember that you are doing something that is good for your child, but that is also very hard for her. If you remain calm, it makes it easier for your child to also regain her equilibrium faster.

> Zoe had a fear of loud noises. She would startle easily and hated the feeling of hearing anything loud. Her parents, Judy and Erik, tried to help by warning if there was going to be a sudden noise. They would tell her before turning on the air conditioner, or when they tested the smoke alarm in their home. But Zoe's fears increased to the point that she would become upset at noises even if she was warned in advance. She was not able to attend birthday parties because of the balloons that could pop, or to go to her brother's football games because of the noise of the crowd. Judy and Erik felt badly for Zoe and were concerned that she seemed to be avoiding more and more things. When they made their accommodation map, they were amazed at how many things they were doing differently because of Zoe's fear and sensitivity. Talking it over, they noticed all the small ways that they had become accustomed to accommodating. They would never turn on the garbage disposal in the sink until after Zoe was asleep because of the noise it made. They kept their phones on silent so they wouldn't ring out loud, and they were even careful never to put the phone down on a table or desk because even vibrating would make a sound. Erik realized it had been months since he had checked the smoke alarms, and they realized they were keeping the air conditioner off even when the day was hot. They would try to stop the microwave just before it went off because of the pinging sound. They even tried to get Zoe's sister to talk softly at home, though this was usually not successful. Their joke together was that no matter how heated an argument they had, at least they would never raise their voices or slam a door.

Judy and Erik made an accommodation plan that included using the garbage disposal whenever there was garbage in the sink, turning on their phone ringers, and checking the smoke alarms every week. They let Zoe know what they were planning and why they were doing it. Zoe didn't say much in response and seemed very quiet and withdrawn for the hour or two after they gave her the message.

Judy and Erik decided that even though their plan included turning on the phone ringers, they would wait to do that until they had practiced once or twice with the garbage disposal and smoke alarm first. They wanted to be able to decide when the first steps in the plan took place and didn't want to be surprised by the phone ringing. The next day after dinner Judy was washing up and knew the time had come. She thought about reminding Zoe of the plan before turning on the garbage disposal but decided they had already told her and that she would just go for it. She turned on the disposal and held her breath to see what would happen. Zoe, who had been sitting nearby in the living room reading, jumped. She got up and ran to her room. The disposal ran for under a minute but Zoe stayed in her room. She was still there 40 minutes later when Judy went to her. She was not sure whether Zoe was upset, scared, or angry with her and was apprehensive about a confrontation. Judy knocked softly on the door and poked her head inside. Zoe was on her bed reading. She looked at Judy and went back to her book. Judy said, "I just want to say I'm proud of you Zoe. I know the noise was unpleasant for you, and I'm proud you were able to cope with it." Zoe didn't respond and Judy left her alone. When it was bedtime Erik went to tell Zoe to get ready for bed and was able to talk with her normally. He made some of his usual jokes and Zoe laughed with him.

The next afternoon Erik told Zoe he had to check the smoke alarms. This time Zoe got angry. "NO!" she said, "You can't do that to me. I know you're just doing it on purpose because of your stupid plan. You wouldn't even be doing it if it weren't for me, so just don't!" Erik told her he knew she disliked the noise, but that safety was important and that he knew she'd be fine. Zoe clamped her hands over her ears, and Erik tested all the smoke alarms in the house. When he finished, Zoe was crying.

She remained very upset for the rest of the day and did not talk at all at dinner. When Erik activated the garbage disposal after dinner, Zoe yelled at her parents, "Why are you doing these things? Are you going to make all the noises in the world now?" and again stormed to her room.

The first time, the change is new and unfamiliar. You and your child are both experimenting and learning a new set of rules. Soon you both will be used to the change, and it will become easier. Your child might need a few times to become convinced that you are going to stick with your plan. There have probably been plans and rules that you experimented with in the past that didn't end up sticking. For example, have you ever tried to use a sticker chart and forgotten about it after a few days? Or assigned your child a chore but then taken back the responsibility because it was not happening? Or perhaps you've made a resolution about yourself, but only carried it out a few times before giving it up? Your child knows that doing something once doesn't always mean it will be a new permanent rule. He may expect that if change proves hard, you will go back to the old way of accommodating. Once your child sees you sticking with the plan consistently, even if he clearly doesn't like it, he will know that the change is here to stay.

It also will get easier after a few times for another reason. Your child's anxiety will be going down! The first time you don't accommodate, your child may be upset, but once he calms down (and he will!) he will have had a wonderful new experience—the experience of being able to calm *himself*. This ability to regulate his own anxiety is the thing your anxious child needs most. You will have given him a taste of it by not accommodating that one time. But doing something once doesn't make it easy right away. That takes practice and repetition. After you've stuck with the plan for a while and your child has repeatedly calmed himself without your help, he'll begin to feel less vulnerable to becoming anxious, and that is the key to being less anxious.

Stay Supportive

As you continue to implement your plan—consistently reducing or stopping the target accommodations—it is as important as ever to keep up your supportive responses. In fact, your supportive statements now take on a whole new level of meaning and impact. Now that you are reducing the accommodation, you're not just telling your child how strong she is and that you have confidence in her—you're showing it! Every time you don't provide the accommodation, you're telling your child in the most powerful way, "I believe in you" and "I know you can do this!"

Your child knows that you would never expect him to do something he is not capable of. For example, think about how a child learns to ride a bike. Someone, often the mother or father, will hold the child at first and then will let go. When you let go of the bike, it's because even though your child doesn't know how to ride right now, you are confident that he will be able to learn the skill. You wouldn't place a baby on a bike and let go. That would be absurd because you wouldn't have confidence that the baby is able to learn to ride, and when he falls, it would be cruel and pointless. When your child is older and is learning to ride, you do let go. You know there is a good chance he will fall, but the fall is no longer pointless. It's an unpleasant step on the way to mastering a new capability. The difference is not in the fall, but rather in your belief about what your child is able to do.

When you let go of the accommodation, you know your child may have some discomfort, just like when you let go of the bike. But your confidence in your child's ability to cope with anxiety makes the unpleasantness temporary and worthwhile. Your child will also understand that you would not let go of the accommodation unless you really do believe that he can cope. So reducing the accommodation makes supportive statements much more real.

Try to make as many supportive statements as you can! As your child is adjusting and developing her own internal ability to better reduce anxiety, she will see that you understand the difficulty of feeling anxious and that you believe she can handle it.

Praise

Give your child a lot of praise and positive reinforcement for handling the change in your accommodation. It will let her know that you understand it's a tough challenge (another way of showing acceptance). Praise is also a good way to remind your child that you are making these changes to help her and not because you are punishing her for being anxious or seeking accommodation. After all, parents are much more likely to praise their children for doing something well than for having completed a punishment. By giving your child a lot of praise and encouragement you will be making it clear that you are on her side and fighting for her so that she can become less anxious.

Remember that you are praising your child for coping and getting through the difficulty of you not accommodating, not for actually doing (or not doing) something himself. This means that you will almost always be able to find something to praise in your child! Whether he took the reduced accommodation in stride—perhaps making an effort to cope on his own—or whether he responded with difficulty and distress, you can praise him for coping and getting through the difficult situation.

Praise from other people, apart from parents, also can be very meaningful to a child. In Chapter 12, you will read about how other people who know you and your child can be instrumental in helping you to cope supportively if your child responds with difficulty to the changes in your accommodation. But even when things are going smoothly, people from outside the immediate family can be helpful in providing praise for your child, acknowledging the difficulty she is coping with and praising her for getting through it. Consider asking a grandparent or an aunt or uncle, or perhaps a family friend or more distant relative, to reach out to your child and let her know how proud they are of her. A brief phone call, a text message, or a short statement during a visit to the house, can be very impactful. It will show your child that the people who care about her are there cheering her on, and this additional support can motivate her to make an even bigger effort to overcome her anxiety.

You can also use rewards to show your child that you are proud of him for coping. Small prizes, treats, or other little things are preferable to big things. A small token or treat indicates that you are still moving forward in an ongoing process, whereas a big prize is usually more suited to having completed a process and reached its end. You'll also be able to give many more rewards if you keep them small. It's the message you are conveying to your child by rewarding him, rather than the size of the reward, that makes the gesture meaningful.

Success for You Means You Didn't Accommodate

Keep your focus on your own behavior, and don't expect your child's behavior to change right away. For now, success means that you didn't accommodate. Overcoming anxiety takes time, and for now, the focus is on what *you* are doing. If you stick with your plan, give your child a lot of support, and reduce your accommodation, you will probably soon see that your child's anxiety is getting better. But don't expect the change to happen overnight. At first, you may even feel as though your child's anxiety is getting worse. This can happen because your child has been used to relying on accommodation when he feels anxious and has not yet become accustomed to coping on his own. Give your child some time and have confidence that he does have the capacity to cope—he just needs more opportunities to discover that capacity in himself.

Parker was seven years old and had a phobia of elevators. Ever since he heard a story about a person being trapped in an elevator, he was unable to ride—or even step into—an elevator, no matter how high up he was going. At first it was not a big deal, but when he started going to a local chess club on the sixth floor of a high-rise building, his fear of elevators became a problem. He would not ride the elevator up or down, and his parents were frustrated about having to walk all those steps with him twice a week. The problem became even bigger when Parker started to avoid other closed places and insisted on keeping an open door wherever he was. His parents, Lucy and Carlos, planned to stop the accommodation of walking up to the chess club. At first, they focused their efforts on the way up, because they knew Parker really loved the club and would want to get there. They were less confident about what would happen on the way out and wanted to avoid getting stuck up there or having a scene in front of his teacher or the other kids. They let Parker know about the plan and told him they understood that elevators were scary for him, but they were sure he could handle it and would be with him all the way.

When they got to the chess club building for the first time after telling Parker their plan, the child headed straight for the steps. Lucy reminded him about the plan and pushed the elevator button. Parker stayed on the first step and did not join his mother. When the elevator arrived, Lucy got in and held the door for him, but Parker still would not come. In the end she rode up without him and he took the stairs.

Lucy felt that the plan had not worked. She had not accommodated by walking up with Parker, but he still did not take the elevator.

What do you think about what happened with Parker and his mother? Is Lucy correct that the plan failed? If success means that Parker takes the elevator, then, of course, this was not yet a success. But the plan was not for Parker to take the elevator. The plan was for *Lucy to not* take it, and by this standard, the event was successful. Lucy managed not to accommodate, and she stayed positive and supportive with Parker. Even though the ultimate goal is for Parker to be less scared and to be able to ride in elevators with his parents, that will take some time. It's reasonable to expect that Parker still will choose not to take the elevator, because, after all, he remains scared of it. Focusing on what Parker is doing, rather than on her own behavior, is causing his mother to feel frustrated and disappointed. Feeling that way will make it harder for her to persist with her plan. Reminding herself that the plan was always about what she is going to do will make it easier for Lucy to persevere even if the change in Parker's behavior comes more slowly.

Success for Your Child Means Getting Through It

Don't wait for your child to show that she is less anxious before giving her praise or rewards. You can praise her for coping even if she is still having a hard time or, like Parker, is still anxious and avoidant. The harder it is for your child to cope without the accommodation, the more praise she deserves for having done so.

Thinking about your child's success at this stage as getting through the difficult moment without accommodation, gives you something special. It gives you the power to "force" your child to succeed. If you don't accommodate and your child gets through it— she is successful! Make good use of this power; it's not often you have the ability to guarantee that your child will succeed at something. Most of the time, we think of success for a child as something that happens when the child does something well. For example, if a child gets a good grade or wins a game, we say that she succeeded.

But we can't ensure that she will do those things; we can only give her the tools and encourage her to do her best. When you don't accommodate your anxious child, you can make sure that she'll succeed because all she has to do is get through a tough situation. No matter how she does that, it will be a success.

Dominic's mother, Angelina, had been accommodating his separation anxiety. She would lie next to him at night until he fell asleep and would never leave him alone in the house. Dominic was 12 years old, and Angelina thought he was old enough to be alone for a while, but Dominic would not even agree to stay home with a babysitter. If Angelina really needed to go out, she would call her sister to come over because she was the only other person with whom Dominic would agree to stay. If Angelina tried to leave the boy alone even for a few minutes, or to get a different babysitter, he would cry and cling to her. She thought his behavior was immature but had been at a loss over how to solve the problem.

Angelina made a plan to go out for ten minutes every other evening. Ten minutes was not enough time to get anything done, but she didn't feel as though she could start with a longer separation. She also wanted to be able to practice her plan several times a week and knew that would be hard to manage with a longer outing. Dominic cried when she told him the plan. He told her he couldn't do it, and that if she loved him, she would not leave him alone; nonetheless, Angelina remained firm.

Later that evening, Angelina was ready to go out for the first time. She told Dominic she would be back in ten minutes and headed for the door. Dominic ran to the door and tried to block it. Angelina wasn't sure what to do, and she decided to try to leave anyway and managed to go around him. Dominic was crying and tried to hold on to her foot. Angelina barely managed to leave the house. She felt angry at Dominic for his behavior and guilty for having made him feel so bad. Angelina used the ten minutes to walk around the block a couple of times. By the time she got back she was feeling calmer, but she was nervous about how Dominic would behave when she went inside. She imagined him still

*lying on the floor near the door and crying. She was also worried that he
would be angry at her or that he truly felt that leaving meant she didn't
love him anymore.*

*When Angelina got inside, Dominic was on the couch. He was
playing on his iPad, but Angelina could see he had been crying a lot.*

What do you think Angelina said to Dominic when she got home?
What would you have said? Should she reprimand him for blocking
her path to the door? Or for acting immature? Should she apologize
to the boy for putting him in a situation that made him so anxious
that he behaved this way? Should she reassure him that she loves
him despite going out? Or should she simply ignore what happened
and try to move on so his mood will improve?

Any of these would be natural responses, but Angelina had a great
opportunity here. Rather than focusing on how difficult the situation
had been, or on how Dominic had behaved, Angelina could focus on
the amazing thing that just happened. Dominic stayed by himself at
home for ten minutes! For the first time in their memory, Dominic had
coped with his fear. He had made it through the ten minutes without
accommodation, and had even managed to calm himself enough to
play his game on the iPad. This was a huge step forward. Now Dominic
knows that his mother thinks he's strong enough to handle the anxiety of being without her. And he knows that it is possible for him to
calm down without her help. It may still not be easy the next time,
but he'll never have to do it for the first time again! Realizing what a
step forward it was for Dominic, Angelina could say something like,
"Dominic, I'm so proud of you right now!! You did it!" By sticking
with her plan, Angelina guaranteed that Dominic would succeed.

Feeling Ready and Being Ready

*I once met with a young man, Quan, who was about to leave for
college and was feeling terrified of leaving home and growing up. He*

had been looking forward to college and had gotten into the school of his choice, but now that it was almost time to go, he felt as if he had cold feet. I met with Quan several times and he kept repeating, "I don't think I'm ready for this." His anxiety was so strong that he would get a panic attack just from thinking about going to college. Any time one of his parents would discuss some preparation that needed to be done, such as buying supplies for his dorm room or packing up clothes, he would feel completely overwhelmed and break down in tears. In the end Quan went off to college and within a week, he felt at home. He made friends, joined a club, and did well in his classes. Much later I spoke with him again, and he told me there was one thing we discussed during those meetings that he remembers helping him to go: "You don't need to feel ready to go—you just need to be ready!"

Being ready and feeling ready are two very different things. Getting settled in college and adjusting to his new schedule showed Quan that he actually had been ready, he just hadn't felt it. We don't always know what we're ready for until we actually do it. Have you ever been anxious yourself about starting something new, such as a new job? Or perhaps when you first became a parent you weren't sure you were ready to take on that role and responsibility. Many new parents feel that way, and most of us will have doubted our readiness at one time or another. Not feeling ready is not a good indication of whether you actually are ready. It's just an indication of how anxious something makes you. If nobody did anything until they felt completely ready, we wouldn't be able to do much at all.

Your child may not be feeling ready yet to cope without your accommodation. This is not a sign that she's actually not ready; it's just a sign that it makes her anxious. As you continue to implement your plan, your child will see that even if she doesn't feel ready—she actually is.

Taking Another Step Forward

Once you have been able to carry out your plan and reduce the accommodation consistently, it may be time to take the next step. If you have been reducing accommodation to a partial degree, it might be time to raise the bar to the next level. For example, if you've been limiting how much time you will stay in your child's room when he goes to sleep, it might be time to lower that further. Or if you've limited how many worry questions you are going to answer, it could be time to stop altogether, or further lower the number. If you already completely removed one accommodation, it might be time to take on another. Either way, follow the same process as the first time around:

- *Monitor.* If you've been partially reducing an accommodation, review your log to see how that has been going. If you are thinking of taking on another accommodation, go back to your general accommodation map and think about which would be another good target. Remember that it's best if you choose something that happens frequently, to give you and your child plenty of opportunity for practice.
- *Plan.* Think through the details of the plan. What changes will you make, and how will you make them? What will you do instead? Are there any challenges you can think of that will make it harder for you to do this? What solutions do you have?
- *Let your child know.* Tell your child what you're planning. Start with a supportive statement, and check that you are giving the *why, what, when, who,* and *how and how much* of your plan.

But what if you've been having difficulty implementing your plan? Chapter 12 and Chapter 13 deal with challenges that parents face in reducing accommodation. You'll learn about some of the difficulties other parents have encountered and about useful strategies for overcoming them.

In This Chapter You Learned About:

- Keeping a log of your progress
- What to expect as you begin reducing the target accommodation
- How to continue to be supportive
- What success means both for you and for your child
- The difference between feeling ready and being ready
- Taking another step

12

Troubleshooting—Dealing with Difficult Child Responses

Your Child Becomes Aggressive When You Don't Accommodate

Trinity was 14 years old, and had a very strong fear of being exposed to poison or hazardous chemicals. She was extremely careful with what she ate, insisting that her parents only buy food from one or two specific stores, and she never ate anything outside of her home. One day she heard a news story about the air quality in her town and became constantly preoccupied with exposure to "bad air." Trinity's parents, Kevin and Nevaeh, were used to accommodating Trinity's fears, but her fear of air pollution pushed them to their limit. They purchased an air purifier for their home, but this ended up having a negative effect because now Trinity would not allow them to open a window. Trinity would actively check to make sure all the windows in the home were closed as soon as she got home from school and would be angry if anyone opened one. Kevin and Nevaeh would air out the house while their daughter was out, but to avoid having a fight with her they would tell her the windows had been closed the whole time.

Their accommodation plan involved opening the windows in their bedroom, the kitchen, and the living room. They decided to allow Trinity to maintain control over the window in her own bedroom, thinking it would give her a place to go if she was too scared to be in the rest of house and because they hoped it would show her that they were not simply trying to make her uncomfortable.

Giving Trinity the message with the plan was very difficult. Kevin and Nevaeh chose a time when they hoped that everyone would be calm, but things rapidly began to go downhill. Kevin began by telling Trinity, "We know you worry a lot about things like air quality and pollution," but he was not able to complete the sentence because Trinity interrupted saying, "You don't know anything, you're not me." Kevin tried again. "That's true, we can't know exactly what it's like, but we understand that it's hard," and again Trinity interrupted with, "Stop saying you understand! You don't understand, so don't say that! Why are you even here? What do you want from me?"

At this point Nevaeh intervened saying, "OK, Trinity, maybe you're right, but there is something we want to tell you, and we've thought a lot about it. Will you let us say it, please? Then we promise to go if you want." Trinity shrugged but remained quiet so Nevaeh continued. "We believe that you can cope with your fears and that us going along with them—not opening the windows in the house—is not helpful or good for you. We decided to make a change to our behavior so we can help you better." Trinity jumped up from her bed and yelled, "You better not open them! Don't you dare. This proves that you don't understand anything at all. I can't breathe that shit! I'm warning you, don't even think about it!"

Kevin and Nevaeh tried to get through the rest of their message so that Trinity would know exactly what they intended, but they didn't believe she heard them at all. Trinity was yelling and, uncharacteristically for her, she was swearing. They didn't recall ever seeing her so angry. They left a written copy of their message in her room and left the room, feeling anxious themselves about what would happen next. Trinity took the written message and put it on their bed with a big red X.

The next day, when she got home from school, Trinity rushed to look around the house and check all the windows. She saw that the windows in the kitchen and living room were open part way and flew into a rage. Nevaeh wasn't home yet, but Kevin was, and Trinity stormed toward him yelling, "Why did you do it?! I told you I can't breathe this shit!" Kevin said, "Trinity, I know it's hard, but you'll be OK. And please don't use that kind of language." Trinity yelled back, "Language? You're poisoning me and you care about my language? Shit, shit, shit, shit!!" Kevin said, "Stop it, Trinity. I'm still your father even if you're upset, and we don't talk like that." Trinity, however, seemed to be completely out of control. She closed the windows and continued to yell and to swear.

Kevin tried to ignore her until she said to him, "OK, you made your point. But this better be the last time. I hope you're happy!" Kevin reminded her that their plan was not a one-time thing, saying, "Mom and I are going to continue because that's what we decided." This seemed like the last straw for Trinity. She yelled something incomprehensible and stormed into Kevin's home office, where she swept his things off his desk and threw them on the floor. Kevin came in and said, "Trinity!! What are you doing? Stop that!" Trinity reached toward one of the shelves and Kevin reached out and grasped her hand, at which point she kicked him. Kevin was shocked and Trinity herself seemed taken aback at her own behavior. She left the room and went to her own bedroom, slamming the door. When Nevaeh came home later that afternoon, she also was appalled by what happened. Both parents wondered whether they were making a mistake by opening the windows.

What should Kevin and Nevaeh do next? Their attempt to reduce accommodation has resulted in a disturbing incident, with Trinity acting in uncharacteristically aggressive ways. She is yelling at her parents, swearing, threatening them, and she even kicked her father— something she never did before. Unsurprisingly, the parents are wondering whether they have made a mistake by not agreeing to continue the accommodation and keep the windows closed. They certainly don't want to turn an anxious daughter into one who is both anxious and violent. And what should they do about her behavior? Can they overlook the fact that Trinity has behaved in an unacceptable manner? Doesn't there have to be a consequence for such behavior? And if they don't impose some consequence, aren't they condoning violence and bad language?

If your child reacts aggressively to your plan not to accommodate, don't be too alarmed. Remember the "fight" half of "fight or flight" from Chapters 1 and 10? Trinity has not suddenly turned into a violent girl who is going to behave aggressively in all circumstances. If your child is typically aggressive, and this has been an ongoing problem, then reducing your accommodation of her anxiety is probably not going to solve the aggression problem. But if your child is not usually aggressive, and the behavior is not typical, then reducing your accommodation is very unlikely to change that. It is far more likely that your child is simply reacting to your decision to override her wishes in a way that makes her feel anxious or scared.

Continuing with a plan to reduce accommodation is unlikely to make your child more aggressive over time. In fact, it is the opposite. Stopping the plan because your child has acted aggressively is *more* likely to lead to more aggressive behavior in the future. Why is that? Because your child will have learned that acting aggressively is an effective way of shaping your behavior. Teaching your child that violence and aggression are the way to get people to do what she wants is probably not the lesson you are trying to teach her.

Should You Punish Your Child for the Aggression?

Punishing your child for reacting with aggression to the change in accommodation is not useful. Punishments exist to make it less likely that a behavior will repeat itself. In the case of an aggressive reaction to reduced accommodation, you don't need punishment to achieve that goal. If you continue with your plan despite your child's behavior, he will see that acting this way is not working. As your child becomes more accustomed to the change in your behavior, he won't have such a strong reaction to it. His anxiety will be going down, and the aggression will most likely stop on its own.

Try to remember that your child is acting aggressively in response to something you did. Frustration and anxiety both lead to aggression. Your child is frustrated because his expectation has not been met, and he is anxious because he has an anxiety problem that is being challenged. It is reasonable for your child to have the expectation that you will behave as you have in the past, and not doing so can cause him to feel frustration. Once you've persisted for a few times, however, your child will no longer have the expectation that you will accommodate, and he will be less frustrated when you don't. He will also be less anxious as he becomes accustomed to the new situation and gets better at regulating his own fear. That will make it less likely that he will act aggressively, even with no punishment from you.

Here are some phrases you can use to remind yourself of your goal and stay calm:

- My child is acting this way because she is anxious. I don't want to punish anxiety.
- My child will get used to this soon—it won't be this hard forever.
- I want to keep the focus on the anxiety—not make this about bad behavior.
- Even though it's hard, I'm helping my child.
- By staying calm I can show my child that I am in control.
- By staying calm I'm showing my child that I am not afraid of his anxiety.

But What about the Next Time? Won't Your Child Be Aggressive Again?

It is possible that your child will act aggressively again, but as explained in the next few sections, there are some things you can do to make it less likely.

Don't Agree to Argue

Look back at the interaction between Kevin and Trinity when she came home and discovered the windows were open. Trinity is immediately upset and angry, but she does not go straight to her father's home office to throw things on the floor, nor does she immediately become physically aggressive. There is a process leading up to those behaviors. At first, to show her father how angry she is, Trinity uses a bad word that she knows is sure to get a reaction from him. He responds to her, reminding her of the plan not to accommodate and telling her not to use bad language. Next, Trinity escalates the argument by repeating the word several times, and Kevin again reprimands her. Trinity continues to rage, and when she demands that they not repeat the window opening, her father tells her that they do intend to continue, at which point Trinity takes the next step and attacks his office. Kevin attempts to intervene, and the fight culminates in him physically trying to stop her from causing more damage and in Trinity kicking him.

Is there anything Kevin could have done differently that might have made it likelier for the situation to end with less aggression? Probably! Kevin could have chosen not to respond to Trinity at all. At multiple points during the interaction, Kevin could have chosen not to agree to argue. Think back to the ping-pong metaphor from Chapter 10 and how parents can choose not to play. When Trinity asks her father to promise that they won't open the windows again, she is clearly challenging him, saying, "This better be the last time." Kevin and Nevaeh have already informed Trinity of their plan (and demonstrated their intent to act on it) and there is no need to remind her again. Instead of rising to the challenge, Kevin could choose to ignore the statement completely. Kevin could also choose not to address Trinity's bad language at that moment. Kevin probably felt it his duty to tell his daughter not to swear, but by addressing her language in that moment, he was also keeping the argument going. Not addressing the language in that moment does not have to mean not addressing it at all. If he felt it was important enough, Kevin could always return to the issue later, when it would not prolong an argument over the accommodation. But it may be best to simply ignore it, and choose to keep his focus on the anxiety instead.

Even when Trinity threw Kevin's things on the floor, his reaction probably led to more aggression rather than less. She had already attacked his desk when he entered the office and reprimanded her, telling her to "stop that." This ended up having the opposite effect from what he wanted, leading Trinity to also reach for his shelves. And finally, although kicking her father was a shocking behavior for both of them, it only occurred when he physically grasped her arm to restrain her.

The point here is not to blame Kevin for Trinity's behavior. His reactions were reasonable, and her behavior is not his fault. But choosing not to argue would likely have resulted in less escalation and aggression than what actually happened. If your child is reacting with aggression, ask yourself whether it is truly necessary for you to respond, or can you simply ignore the behavior? Try to notice the conflict growing before it reaches the boiling point, and you can choose not to participate. If you are able to withdraw before things escalate, there's a good chance they won't.

Focus on Your Behavior

Reducing aggression is one of the biggest advantages of focusing on your own behavior rather than on your child's. If you have refrained from providing an accommodation, your job in that situation is done. If the focus was on your child's behavior, then you wouldn't be able to end the situation successfully until you ensured that your child did what you expect. Then you'd have no choice but to argue. But remember, you are not trying to make your child do something. Kevin has no need to argue with Trinity, because he is not requiring anything of her. Kevin, of course, hopes that their plan will cause Trinity to eventually become less worried about the air quality and less avoidant of open windows. For now, however, the plan does not involve Trinity. Having opened the windows himself, Kevin has accomplished what he set out to do and has no need to argue with Trinity. Choosing not to respond to Trinity when she challenged him never to open the windows again would not have made that situation any less of a success.

Get Some Help

If you are concerned about your child being aggressive when you don't accommodate, consider enlisting the help of another person. Having someone else around next time you implement your plan will make it much less likely that things will get out of hand. Most children will behave better in front of other people than they will in front of just their parents and siblings. It's human nature to be a bit more inhibited when more people can see us. Is there a friend or a relative or a neighbor you can ask to come over? You may find that having another person around will also help you to not escalate the argument.

You may feel uncomfortable about asking for someone else's help; or, you may be embarrassed about your child's behavior, and this is understandable. Try to think of someone you trust and explain to them that you and your child are working through something difficult and that they can help. Would you want to help your friend if they asked you? Or would you judge them for having a challenge? Most people appreciate being asked for help. They feel honored by the request and they admire parents who are working to help their child overcome a challenge. You are doing something praiseworthy by making an effort to help your child be less anxious.

Even if you are not able to have another person around when you reduce the accommodation, other people can still help if your child reacts aggressively. Ask someone who knows your child to talk to her and tell her they understand how hard it must be to be coping with fear or anxiety, but they also know that she acted aggressively. If your child gets a supportive message that shows her that she is not being criticized or blamed, but that others know about the aggression and are concerned, she is far less likely to repeat the behavior.

Your Child Is So Upset—This Feels Like Torture!

Seeing how much your child is suffering can be so hard! You love your child and want him to feel good. But here you are, actually causing him to feel uncomfortable, and if this feels like torture, that's not surprising. Remember that as a parent your brain is programmed to recognize signs of anxiety in your children and to want to act in their defense. Also recall how anxiety takes over your child's healthy fear system and turns it into something that gets in the way. The same thing can happen to you as a parent. Your healthy and natural desire to help your child to be less stressed or anxious can actually get in the way of helping your child become less anxious.

Anxiety: What Goes Up Must Come Down

Do you remember Angelina from Chapter 11? She left her child, Dominic, with separation anxiety at home and went outside for ten minutes. Those ten minutes probably felt like an hour of torture for Angelina. But by the time she got home, her son was already much calmer, and she was able to praise him for having stayed alone for the first time. Your child's distress may not pass in ten minutes, but *it will pass*. As the saying goes, what goes up must come down. When your child's anxiety levels shoot up and his brain activates the fight or flight system, his body is also working on bringing those levels of anxiety back down. Anxiety goes down much more slowly than it goes up, so it may take a while until your child is calm again, but he'll get there.

The Traffic Light

Whenever parents say something to me along the lines of, *"My child has panic attacks that last for hours,"* or *"My kid will cry and beg for hours and hours,"* my first question is: What are you doing during those hours? Almost invariably, these parents are trying to help their child get calm, or to explain to the child why the parent is not accommodating. It seems paradoxical, but most of the things you do to help your child feel better when you are not accommodating are actually going to keep her anxiety levels high for longer than if you let her cope on her own. The reason is not that the things you are doing cause anxiety, but that as long as you are trying to help, your child will have more difficulty accepting that you won't accommodate.

If your child is repeatedly asking you for an accommodation, then continuing to tell him "no" is likely to prolong the discussion and drive his anxiety and frustration higher. In Chapter 10, I used the example of arguing over buying your child an expensive Rolex watch to illustrate how your child is likely to believe there's a chance you'll change your mind as long as you are arguing. It can seem strange that the thing you're doing to help him stop a behavior can actually have the opposite result, but in reality that kind of thing happens a lot.

Consider something as commonplace as a traffic light, which has a very simple job. Traffic lights tell drivers when to go, when to stop, and when to slow down because the signal is about to change. We know that red means "stop," and green means "go," but what about yellow? If you are approaching an intersection and the light is yellow, the message is supposed to be, "Slow down, because you won't make it through." But have you ever noticed that this is not what many drivers do when they see a yellow light? It's typical to see drivers speed up when the light is yellow, and this is exactly the opposite of what the light is signaling (and frequently results in running a red light)! Sometimes, you may think you are giving your child one message while, in fact, she hears the opposite. Your continued responses can be like that yellow light. If your child is having a tough time accepting that you are not providing an accommodation, then repeatedly telling her you are not going to accommodate or doing other things that are intended to help her feel better, can actually make the process longer and harder because your child interprets your responses as a signal to continue, and she speeds up rather than slowing down.

A Time-Limited Experiment

Seeing your child in distress can be hard, but it won't last forever. Even if your plan to reduce accommodation were to not work at all, at some point you would have to try something else. Research shows that reducing your accommodation in a supportive way is very likely to help your child become less anxious, but it would be pointless to continue forever if it didn't have any positive effect. So think about what you're doing as a time-limited experiment. Are you able to practice your plan for a while? Doing it once or twice is not really giving it a chance, but can you do it for a month? Three weeks? Two? If you remind yourself that you don't have to do it forever and that your child will probably be less anxious soon, it may be easier to cope right now.

Your Distress or Your Child's?

Is it possible that some of the discomfort you're feeling is because you are so worried for your child, rather than because she is suffering so much? Do you remember taking your children to get shots at the doctor's office when they were very young babies? Many parents will recall the experience vividly because it was so hard . . . for them. Imagine a parent with a phobia of needles who takes her baby to get a shot. This parent is horrified about exposing her child to such an awful thing. She is so used to seeing needles and shots as terrifying that she might feel less like the doctor is giving the baby a shot and more like the doctor is feeding the baby to a lion! Think about how that parent is going to sit in the chair, tense and stiff as though she just sat down in an electric chair, clutching her baby tightly. Getting a shot can be objectively uncomfortable, and every baby getting the same shot might experience some discomfort. But this experience is worse, not because this baby is different, or because this shot hurts more, but because the parent feels as if she is doing something awful.

If your child seems distressed or distraught by the lack of accommodation, ask yourself how much of what you are experiencing has to do with your own feelings about your child's anxiety. If you and your partner are working on the plan together, or even if you have a partner who is not involved in the plan, you might consider asking them how much they think your child is suffering. Do they see it the same way, or do they have a different view? Regardless of who is more correct, just hearing another perspective might change how you view your child's experience. You could even consider asking your child himself. Once he has calmed down and is less upset, you could ask how bad he thinks that experience was. (Don't ask while he's in the immediate grip of anxiety. That answer is predictable and likely not accurate.) You may be surprised to learn that your child does not consider it to have been as bad as you thought.

Get Some Help

Going through something hard is always a challenge, but doing it alone can make it harder. If you know that not accommodating causes your child a lot of distress or discomfort, try to lean on a friend or relative who can help you get through the tough moments. Having someone over, or talking to someone on the phone, can give you support.

Your Child Threatens Self Harm if You Don't Accommodate

There are not many things a child can say that scare a parent more than a threat of self harm. The idea of your child hurting herself is a parent's nightmare. If your child has threatened to hurt herself if you continue with a plan to reduce accommodation, you are probably feeling scared, worried, and perhaps even angry. It's natural to be frightened because you care so much about your child's safety, and it's normal to feel angry because you may have the sense that you are being manipulated. You may also be unsure about whether to continue with your plan and whether that would be putting your child's safety at risk.

Before you read about how to cope with threats of self harm, there are a few things that are important to know:

1. *Statements* about suicide and self harm among children and adolescents are quite common. Statements such as these can reflect an actual thought or intent to act in a self-harming way. They can also be used to convey how badly a child is feeling, or to compel a parent to act in accordance with the child's wishes.

2. *Thoughts* of self harm are also common in youth. Most children and adolescents who think or talk about harming themselves are not going to do so, but in some cases the statements can indicate real risk.

3. Suicide *attempts* and *suicide* do happen in children and adolescents. Suicide is a leading cause of death in youth and rates have been rising in recent years. Therefore, it is never OK to brush off threats of self harm. If your child has threatened to kill or hurt himself, you should take that threat seriously. Even if your child only makes these statements while angry with you or because you have not accommodated, and the actual risk of self harm is low, you should still take the threat seriously.

Taking a child's threat seriously, however, does not have to mean stopping your plan to reduce accommodation. It means you do your best to make sure your child is safe. If you are concerned about your child's safety, the first thing you should do is seek professional help in person. You can consult with your pediatrician or see a psychiatrist. Or, if the worry is immediate, you can always get help in a hospital emergency room. Once you have gotten help in figuring out the level of risk for your child, you can continue to do your best to keep him safe. You can also continue the work of helping your child overcome his anxiety problem. Reducing your child's anxiety is a positive thing that can lower the real-life risk of self harm.

Dillon was 16 years old and had been struggling with obsessive-compulsive disorder (OCD). His parents, Morgan and Andy, were attempting to reduce their accommodation of always arranging items in the house in accordance with Dillon's OCD. They had decided to start with not always putting books on the bookshelf in alphabetical order. They knew that Dillon would probably just "fix" anything they put on the shelf out of order, but they were determined to show him that they believed he could overcome the OCD. Morgan and Andy were surprised by Dillon's response. The first two times he did just rearrange the books, but the third time he told them they had to stop because he couldn't take it. He picked up a large knife in the kitchen and holding it to his chest, he said, "Do you see? This is what you're making me do if you continue."

Morgan and Andy were surprised and upset. Andy found the threat particularly disturbing because of a history of suicide in his family. His uncle had committed suicide a few years earlier, and then his son, Andy's cousin, had also killed himself. Although he had never had suicidal thoughts himself, Andy feared that there was a tendency to suicide in the family and that his children might be at risk. Seeing Dillon holding a knife to his chest and hearing him say that he would kill himself if the parents did not accommodate the OCD symptoms shook him deeply. Morgan was also concerned, but she didn't think the threat reflected an actual suicidal intent. She knew that Dillon was aware of his father's fear and believed that Dillon was manipulating his father by playing "the suicide card." Both parents agreed that they could not simply ignore what their son had said.

The next day, when Dillon came home from school, his grandmother Colleen was there. He didn't know she was planning a visit and was happy to see her. Colleen greeted him warmly, but then her face became serious. She said, "Dillon, I know you've been coping with OCD, and I'm sorry that you are going through that. I also heard from your mom and dad that yesterday you threatened to hurt yourself with a knife. I want you to know that everyone is very concerned for you because that is a very serious thing to say. I'm going to stay here today until your parents get back, to help keep watch and make sure you're safe. And tomorrow, your grandpa will be here. We love you, and we want to make sure you are OK."

Dillon was taken aback and a little embarrassed. He flushed and told his grandmother, "You don't need to do that." Colleen asked why he thought she didn't need to be there, and he told her he was not really going to hurt himself and that he was just mad at his parents. Colleen said, "I understand that, Dillon, and I'm glad to hear it. But if someone says they will stab themselves that's not something we can ignore. It's too serious for that, so I'm going to stay anyway just to be sure." Colleen checked on Dillon every ten minutes until his parents got back, knocking on his door when he closed it and saying she just wanted to check that he was all right. When Morgan and Andy got back home, Dillon asked them to tell his grandfather that it wasn't necessary for him to come the next day saying, "It's not like I'm actually going to do it." But the parents repeated what Colleen had said about how serious a threat he had made. "It's our responsibility to keep you safe, and if you threaten to hurt yourself we have no choice but to take it seriously. It's not the kind of thing you can just say and think it won't mean anything."

Andy and Morgan continued with their plan that day, putting books on the shelf out of order. Dillon watched them and seemed unhappy about it, but he did not repeat the threat of self harm. The next day, the grandfather came for the afternoon, and Dillon told him, too, that he had not actually meant to harm himself. The grandfather gave him a hug and said, "Oh, I know that, but did you really think your parents were just going to ignore something like that? You know them better than that. And Dillon, I bet you'll beat this OCD thing soon, I'm rooting for you."

Morgan and Andy found a way to do two things at the same time: They acted to protect their son's safety, and they continued helping him overcome his OCD by reducing accommodation. When Dillon threatened to hurt himself if his parents didn't place the books in alphabetical order, he was telling them they had to make a choice: They could either go back to providing the accommodation, or they could take a risk of him hurting himself. If those were really the only two options, then Morgan and Andy would not have felt like they had much of a choice. Of course they wouldn't agree to place Dillon in danger. But they realized that those were not the only options. Quickly putting together a plan for watching over Dillon was both a way of keeping him safe and of showing him that they took the statement seriously. At the same time, the parents were able to continue with their plan of not accommodating and didn't have to give up on helping Dillon with his OCD.

If your child threatens harm to herself, you do not have to make a choice between safety and not accommodating. Ask yourself what has to happen to keep your child safe and do that. You can also, like Morgan and Andy, call on the help of friends and relatives to help you keep watch to make sure your child is OK. If your child retracts the threat like Dillon did, it may be wise to continue with your safety plan nonetheless. This will help your child learn that she cannot make and retract threats of self harm with no consequences, and will make it less likely that she will use the threat again in the future.

You can also pay a visit to an emergency room with your child and explain that you are there because your child made a threat of self harm. Hospitals are used to seeing children and adolescents who have made similar threats and are not likely to assume that your child is at high risk. If you set out for the hospital, it is probably best to go even if your child retracts the threat on the way.

One additional thing to notice in the way Dillon's family responded to his threat is that it was a *supportive* response. He was not blamed or criticized or punished for making the threat. Everyone made it clear that they understand how hard coping with his OCD must be for him, and that they are there out of love, not anger. Dillon may have preferred that they not keep watch over him, but he knew they were doing it because they cared about him. Being wrapped in so much care from his family would likely have lowered the risk of self harm if Dillon actually was feeling depressed or suicidal.

In This Chapter You Learned About:

- Coping with aggressive child responses
- Coping with distressed child responses
- Coping with threats of self harm in your child

13

Troubleshooting—Dealing with Difficulties in Working with Your Partner

Your Partner and You Don't Agree on This

If you are having disagreements with your partner about how to best respond to your child's anxiety, or you are frustrated with each other because you are not implementing your plan in the same way or to the same degree, guess what? You're like most other parents! You probably think that two parents should be on the same page and show your child a unified and consistent approach in your parenting. It would be great if that were always the case, but that's not the reality of parenting for most families. Having a child together is not like a "Vulcan mind meld," where two people telepathically merge into a single entity. You are two people, with different thoughts and ideas, different attitudes and approaches, different personalities, and different ways of handling problems. It's not surprising that most parents have disagreements with and that they get frustrated with each other for doing or thinking differently.

There are, however, things that you have in common. For example,

- You both probably would like your child to be able to cope better, to be less anxious, and to lead a life less impacted by the anxiety problem.
- You also probably would like to help your child achieve those things.

Keep in mind that even though your partner may disagree with you or may do things differently, they probably want those things just as much as you do, and this understanding can help you both stay more positive and turn a bitter argument into a more constructive process. Try asking your partner what it is they would like to achieve and what they're trying to do, and you may realize that you are not as far apart as you thought.

Children's anxiety problems have the potential to really push parents' buttons and to magnify disagreement, frustration, and conflict. Differences of opinion or attitudes that were present (but not all that important) when you were not coping with an anxious child can become a daily source of conflict when your child is anxious. It's a lot like how differences of opinion about how to manage a financial budget can be mildly irritating when money is abundant, but can become a source of real conflict and strife when finances are tighter. When there is enough money for everyone's priorities, then the money "wasted" on your partner's goals is only a little irritating. But when money is tight and spending becomes an either/or situation, every decision has the potential for disagreement.

It's not hard to see why the presence of a very anxious child can make disagreements about how to cope with the anxiety a major issue between parents. A child's anxiety can have a big impact on the child's life, making parents care deeply about the problem and causing disagreement to be all the more upsetting. A child's anxiety can also impact the lives of the parents and the rest of the family, adding even more to the level of discord. If your child is highly anxious it probably requires you to respond frequently through accommodation or other attempts to help. That means there are many decisions you constantly make about how to handle the anxiety, and with so many opportunities to do things one way or another, it's easy to see how disagreement can take a front row seat.

Feelings of guilt and blame also can contribute to the anxiety issue becoming an extra-sensitive topic. If you think you have contributed to your child being anxious, or if you believe your partner's behavior is to blame, then talking about the anxiety and working together becomes much harder. Or, if you perceive that your partner is blaming you for your child's anxiety, it's hard not to feel hurt, angry, or indignant. So don't be surprised if you find that working together on the steps in this book, or coping with the anxiety in general, places some strain on your relationship.

Having met many parents of children coping with anxiety, I know there is not much that these parents have in common. Anxious children have parents of all kinds: economically well off and financially struggling, highly educated and not highly educated, strict and permissive, fun loving and serious. There really isn't a family "type" for having an anxious child. *One thing that I have seen again and again, however, is how much having an anxious child can challenge parents' abilities to work cooperatively together.* This does not mean, that parents can't find ways to work together, or that if you and your partner are not in perfect agreement, you won't be able to help your child. If that were so, then most parents would not be able to help much. Or put another way, if the steps in this book were only useful for parents who always agree and have no difficulty making plans together and carrying them out in perfect harmony, then this book wouldn't really be very helpful. Fortunately that is not the case!

There are steps you can take to improve your working relationship around your child's anxiety. Even if you can't agree in the end, and you realize you are going to do it without your partner's collaboration, *you* can still help your child. So try some of these suggestions for things that have helped other parents to overcome difficulties in working together.

Greta and Louis were feeling pretty fed up. Their son Paul was eight years old and had been sleeping in their bed for over a year. There had been what seemed like a brief period when he was six and seven when Paul had slept in his own bed. He would sometimes come to their room in the early morning, but mostly he stayed in bed. Then he started coming in earlier and earlier and soon he was spending all night every night in his parents' bed. Greta and Louis still put Paul to bed in his own room, but he would feel scared alone in bed and within a few minutes he would come to them. If his parents weren't in bed yet, he would cry and one of them would stay near him in his room until he fell asleep. They tried putting a night light in his room, but that didn't help. One of their friends suggested a white noise machine, but that didn't make any difference either. No matter what they did, Paul didn't feel able to stay alone and insisted that he couldn't sleep without them. Greta tried staying with Paul in his bed, but it was small and she felt if she was going to have to be there, she may as well be in her own bed with Paul.

Paul's anxiety had taken a toll on his parents' relationship. They felt as if they had no place to themselves and even after a long day of work and taking care of their three children, they didn't get to relax or spend time on their own together. They also were becoming increasingly frustrated with each other. They knew that Paul really did feel scared in his bed, but they had different ideas on how to handle this, and it seemed as though their day was sandwiched between irritation and disagreement. Louis would lie in bed feeling annoyed, and when they woke up in the morning with Paul right there next to them, the feelings would often boil over into arguments.

Louis believed that their job as parents was to make the rules and that Paul had to follow the rules even if he didn't like it. He was sure that if Paul were not allowed into their bed, he would get used to it, but Louis saw how time kept passing without anything changing. "Do you want him to be sleeping in our bed when he's ten?" he would ask, "Or what about fifteen?!" Louis had tried several times to make Paul stay out of their room, but he felt Greta always sabotaged his efforts. When Paul would come to their room, his mom would always relent and allow him to stay, even after Louis had told the child to stay in his own bed. Louis felt as though Greta was not only keeping Paul from overcoming his fear, she was also undermining Louis's authority as a parent.

Greta thought Louis was being unreasonable. "Of course he'll survive if we don't let him come to our room," she acknowledged, "but what will that do to him? He'll see that even when we know he's scared we're not willing to help." Greta also thought Louis was being unfair to her. It didn't seem right for him to lay down the law and expect her to go along with it when he knew she disagreed with him. "I don't want to undermine you," she told Louis, "but you can't just decide on your own. I want our child to be able to count on us when he's scared, not to lie in bed thinking nobody cares." But Louis felt she was giving him no alternative. "If you're never willing to make a change, then how can I decide with you? I'm all for doing it together, but you never try anything! That's why it's been a year and a half and Paul is still in our bed. Gabrielle is a year younger, and she has sleepovers with her friends. Paul can't have a sleepover because he's not willing to sleep in a bed without us! That's what letting him stay in our bed has done for him."

Tips for Better Communication With Your Partner

Are You Picking the Right Time to Talk?

It's not surprising that Louis and Greta have not yet found a plan on which they both can agree. Their discussions about Paul's anxiety seem to be happening mainly when they are the most frustrated with him and with each other. It's natural for Louis to want to talk about the problem when he wakes up in the morning and feels annoyed and irritated. But feeling that way is probably causing his communication to be much more hostile and conflict-oriented than if he were feeling calmer. Unfortunately, having unproductive conversations or arguments in the morning actually makes both parents less likely to want to talk about the problem at other times. Given that neither parent enjoys the arguments and because they have not yielded positive results, Louis and Greta probably don't want to have even more arguments. So they avoid talking about it at other times when they're not quite as upset and are able to put the issue out of their minds. But this continues the cycle, because the next time one of them is feeling too frustrated to ignore the issue they'll raise it again and probably have another unproductive argument. It's not surprising that over a year has passed without these parents making a plan together!

If you are having a hard time talking to your partner about your child's anxiety, think about *when* you try:

- Are you discussing this when you're angry, upset, or under stress? Or when you are under pressure to respond right then and there? If so, it's not likely to be a great conversation.
- Perhaps you talk about this mainly when one of you has just responded in a way the other disagrees with? That's not going to be a conversation about making a plan; it's more likely to be an argument about who is right and who is wrong.

Try to set aside a time to talk about the issue when neither of you is under pressure nor feeling frustrated and upset. Talking about the problem may raise some of those feelings, but you have a better chance of having a productive conversation if you start out feeling calm. Like Louis and Greta, you also may prefer to avoid talking about the problem unless you really have to, and setting aside a time to discuss it may feel like it adds to the burden. But give it a shot nonetheless. If it helps you to have a more productive conversation, it will feel worthwhile.

Stay Away from Blame

It's easy to point to something one or the other parent is doing as being the cause of the child's anxiety or as the reason the child has yet to overcome her anxiety. But realistically, it's probably wrong! When a child has an anxiety problem, in the vast majority of cases it is *not* because of something a parent is or is not doing. (Of course, extreme forms of negative parenting are harmful to a child's wellbeing. Abuse and neglect, for example, can contribute to child anxiety as well as to other problems. But parents with an anxious child usually have not been abusive or neglectful.) As noted in Chapter 1, it is likely that your anxious child is predisposed to high levels of anxiety through biological and other factors completely outside of your control. So try to stay away from unhelpful blaming and shaming of your partner. If, in talking about the anxiety, you convey that you are trying to "save" your child from your partner's mistakes, then your partner will feel accused and is more likely to be defensive or to accuse you back. And then, the chance of a productive conversation goes way down. When Louis tells Greta that Paul's anxiety is preventing him from having sleepovers and, "That's what letting him stay in our bed has done for him," the implication is that Greta's unwillingness to follow Louis's plan is the reason that Paul is still anxious. When he asks her if she wants Paul to still be sleeping in their bed at the age of fifteen, Louis is suggesting that her choices could be damaging Paul's prospects for years to come. It's no surprise that all this blame does not make Greta feel more open to making a plan together with Louis. Likewise, when Greta asks, "What will that do to him?" in reference to Louis's plan not to allow Paul in their bed, she seems to be suggesting that Louis's plan is harmful and damaging. This probably makes Louis feel less open to working collaboratively with her. Even if you are pointing the finger at yourself, the blame is still inaccurate and unhelpful, and self-blame can make it harder for parents to work together productively.

But Isn't Family Accommodation Bad?

Do you feel as though it's your job to make sure your partner is not accommodating? If you've read this far you know that family accommodation is one factor that can be unhelpful in overcoming childhood anxiety. Of course this doesn't mean that family accommodation is the cause of your child's anxiety. After all, if your child were not anxious, you probably would not be accommodating much, right? Family accommodation is the way parents respond to anxiety, but it is not the thing that causes it. The important thing about accommodation is not that it makes a child anxious—or even keeps him anxious—it's that by reducing accommodation a child can become *less* anxious. Even if accommodation does contribute to child anxiety over time, it is just one factor out of many that will impact the course of your child's anxiety. As you become more and more aware of your own accommodation, it is helpful for you to be working to reduce it and replace it with support. But it's not your job to catch your partner accommodating. Remember that accommodating an anxious child is something that almost every parent will do.

Be Respectful

The way we react to things people tell us is determined as much by the way they say it as by what they say. Have you ever noticed how it's possible to have a whole long argument about something, to feel determined to make your point and get it across at all costs, but then later to realize that you don't even care that much about the whole thing? Or how sometimes you may vehemently deny making a mistake or doing something wrong, but at other times have no difficulty owning the error and even laughing it off? Why would that be? Sometimes it has to do with the mood you happen to be in (and that's why picking the right time to talk matters), and other times it has to do with how you hear what the other person is saying. For example,

- Are they respecting you or putting you down?
- Do they care about your opinion or only about their own?
- Does it seem as if they assume they know better than you do?

These kinds of feelings can put a person in "argument mode." When we're in an argument mode, our focus is not on hearing and considering the points the other person is making, it's on making sure we win the argument. When we're in argument mode, we listen to what the other person is saying not as a way of understanding what they think, but so we can find weak spots that we can challenge and rebut. It's fine to be in argument mode when you're talking for the fun of it, but when you're trying to figure out how to help your child, argument mode doesn't work. It's frustrating to realize that the person you're talking to doesn't really value or consider your opinions, and you may want to end the conversation entirely because it seems pointless.

If you feel that the conversations you have with your partner about your child's anxiety have taken on this frustrating feeling, or that your partner is talking to you in argument mode, try to show them that you value their thoughts and respect their opinion. You may find that your partner is more willing to consider what you have to say if you show them that you don't assume you already know best.

Keep It Focused

When couples have a disagreement, it's hard to keep the focus on just one thing. Two parents have so many things that they need to work out together, and what each of them does impacts the other in so many ways, that things tend to spill over into each other. A discussion about one thing can easily turn into a conversation about any number of other points of contention or dissatisfaction. This does, however, have an unfortunate effect. Because it is unlikely that any conversation will ever resolve *all* of the issues, it makes it very hard to end a discussion without still feeling unhappy or annoyed.

Imagine you go to the dentist because you have a toothache, and on the same day, you are also feeling under the weather. The dentist might do a great job addressing the tooth problem, but you might still be left feeling lousy. Does that mean it was a waste of time to go to the dentist? Or that the dentist didn't do a good enough job? Of course not; she just solved one problem rather than all your problems. If you focus on the issue of

the tooth specifically, you'll probably feel glad that you took care of that.
But if you focus on everything at once and think, "Yes, but I still feel
poorly," you'll probably be disappointed that some problems remain.

This kind of "yes, but" thinking happens a lot in conversations between two parents. You're talking about one issue and then . . . "Yes, but what about that other thing?" It can seem like finding a plan for the one issue is pointless unless you also have solutions for everything, but this is not true. Having one good plan that you can agree on is not only a huge step forward in and of itself, but if you're able to act on it, then it also makes it more likely that you'll be able to agree on other plans for more issues in the future—one at a time.

Try to keep the conversations about how to help your anxious child focused on the issue of the anxiety. In fact, keep your focus on just one specific area of anxiety, rather than all of the things that make your child anxious. If you can put other things aside and just focus on the one issue, it may be easier to come up with a plan for that one specific thing. Note that keeping the focus on one issue can actually be harder than it sounds. Try to listen for those "yes, but" moments when something else is getting mixed into the conversation, making it seem as if doing this one thing won't matter.

Support Means Two Things

Greta and Louis seem to be pretty far apart in their attitudes toward their son's anxiety about sleeping alone. Greta feels it is important for Paul to feel understood and comforted by his parents and to know they stand by him and are ready to help. Louis is adamant about the need for the child to overcome his fear and become better able to handle nights on his own. They both feel that Paul is not getting enough of what he needs. For Greta that is understanding and help, while for Louis it is boundaries and encouragement to cope on his own. At first, it may seem as though there is little hope for these parents to find common ground or to make a plan that will reflect both of their aims.

Recall that supporting a child who is anxious actually means two things: Support happens when parents are able to show their anxious child both acceptance *and* confidence. When we think about what each parent in this case is trying to do, it becomes clearer that they are both advancing an important and necessary aspect of the supportive response. Neither parent can really be supportive without the ingredient of support that the other parent is pushing for:

- Without the confidence in Paul's ability—which is reflected in Louis's expectation that Paul cope on his own—Greta can be accepting and validating of Paul's fear, but she cannot truly be supportive.
- Without the acceptance that is reflected in Greta's understanding that the child is genuinely anxious and that lying alone in bed at night is very hard for him, Louis cannot provide the full recipe for support.

Only putting together the messages that both parents are trying to convey to Paul will result in a complete supportive message. Greta and Louis think they are trapped in a conflict, resisting each other and ultimately undermining one another. In reality, however, Paul needs both ingredients from his parents, and they need each other to craft a supportive message.

If you and your partner find that you disagree about how to respond to your anxious child, or that you are not able to agree on a plan for how to behave, consider whether you have split up the supportive message between the two of you. Very often when two parents disagree about a child's anxiety, it is because each of them is focused on one of the ingredients that combine to make up support. Ask yourself what your partner is trying to achieve, or better yet, ask them! The answer is probably not that your partner is trying to make your child feel worse, or to make him stay more and more anxious. Even if you think your partner has been going about it the wrong way, or has been pigheaded and stubborn by not following your lead, consider that what your partner is trying to do might be an important piece of support that your child needs in order to overcome his fear.

Try Swapping Jobs

When each parent has become focused on only one element of support, it can be helpful to take some time reconnecting with the other, equally critical part of the supportive message. You and your partner can try "swapping jobs"—each taking on the role the other has been filling, for a short period of time. If you are the parent who has been focused on helping your child to feel accepted and understood, try to take time to focus on showing your child that you have confidence that she can handle feeling afraid or worried or anxious some of the time. Practice showing her that you do believe she is strong and not helpless in the face of anxiety. Or, if the job you have taken on has been to be the parent who focuses on making your child cope with her fear and not avoid things because they are hard, try to take time to show your child that you do understand that feeling anxious is hard. Let her know you do realize how uncomfortable the anxiety can make her feel. Below are some questions parents ask about the practice of swapping jobs.

Doesn't Acceptance Mean You Agree that Your Child Can Continue to Avoid Coping?

Not at all. Acceptance means that you understand and acknowledge the difficulty your child experiences. Accepting that something is hard is entirely different from agreeing it should not happen. Even if you have been focused on the importance of coping, you can show your child you realize it's a hard thing.

Doesn't More Confidence Mean Less Acceptance?
No. Confidence in your child means showing him you believe he can tolerate anxiety. It's not confidence in what he will or will not do. (Remember: That's not something you can decide and it's not the focus of your plan.) Confidence means that you believe your child is able to tolerate distress caused by anxiety and that you know he can be OK even if he feels anxious, scared, or worried some of the time.

Can You Change Your Whole Attitude Overnight?
You don't have to! Swapping jobs is something you would only do for a short amount of time, maybe just one day or two. If you try it out for just one instance in which your child is anxious, and act differently than you normally would behave, it can prove very useful. It's also likely that by swapping roles, you are not really doing something that is opposed to what you believe. If your focus has been on acceptance, it's likely that you do want your child to know you believe in her strength and ability. And if you have been focused mostly on confidence, you probably do realize that anxiety is not easy for your child, and you would like her to know that you understand this.

Won't Your Child Be Confused By the Change in Your Reactions?
Maybe, but that's OK. If your child is confused, it just means you are doing something different from what he has come to expect. That's not bad. It is literally impossible to do something *better* without it also being *different*, right? The reason you're swapping jobs is not to cause your child confusion, although it's OK if he is surprised by the change. The reason you're doing this is all about you. By swapping roles and taking on the acceptance instead of only showing confidence, or expressing confidence in place of only showing acceptance, you'll have the chance to reconnect with an ingredient of support that you probably know is important but that has gotten lost in your need to consistently show the other aspect of support.

When one parent feels as though they are the only parent who is expressing confidence, it can start to feel as though they must show *only* confidence, because otherwise, who will? And conversely, if you have felt as though your partner does not express acceptance of your child, you may have become used to feeling as though you must always *only* show as much acceptance as possible, because otherwise your child will not get acceptance from anyone. By swapping jobs for even a short time, you can both get back in touch with the other element of support. You will both have the opportunity to see that your partner is capable of delivering the part of support that you believe they are missing. You may discover this role reversal helps you both come up with a plan that is supportive and that you can agree to implement together.

What Would It Be Like for Greta and Louis to Swap Jobs for a Night?

If for one night Louis decides to focus his efforts on helping Paul to feel better when he's scared, and Greta makes it her goal to help Paul stay in his own bed, what would that look like? Paul, who is used to his mother welcoming him with a reassuring hug, would likely come straight to her side of the bed. But what if on this one night Greta told him, "I see how scared you're feeling, but I think you can be in your bed and still be OK. Come, I'll take you back to bed." Louis could sit up and say, "Paul, wait, let me give you a hug first. I want you to feel better." Regardless of whether Paul ends up sleeping in his own bed, the experiment could have a profound impact on both parents. For Louis, the opportunity to hold Paul and comfort him might be a very meaningful and even emotional moment. For Greta, showing her son that she has confidence in him could actually help her to see him in a different light. And most importantly, for both parents, the swap could help them reconnect with the important goal that their partner is trying to achieve. After swapping roles for a night or two, both parents may find it much easier to work together and to acknowledge that ultimately they are both trying to do their best for their child.

Is There a Plan You Can Agree On?

In Chapter 8 you read about some of the things that make a good target for reducing your accommodation. But even a target that hits all of those points is not very good if it causes you and your partner disagreement. An accommodation that is a less-ideal target, perhaps because it is less frequent or because in your opinion it doesn't interfere as much, might actually be a better target if it is something on which you both can agree. If you have not been able to make a collaborative plan concerning the target you thought was best, try to see if there is something else that you can agree about more. You can always go back and focus on the other accommodation later. Your child will probably be doing better then, because both of her parents have been able to reduce an accommodation together in a supportive way. So don't get too stuck on making a plan for that one specific accommodation, and try to be flexible even if it means taking on a target that is more a reflection of your partner's opinion than your own.

Focus on What You Can Control

By now, you have probably realized that focusing on what you can control, rather than on the things you can't, is a recurring principle in this book. You can't control your child's behavior, and this book has shown you that you don't need to control that to be able to help. You also can't control your partner's behavior, and once again you don't need to be able to do that to help your child. If you've tried all the suggestions in this chapter and have come to the conclusion that there is no way for the two of you to work together at this stage, then it may be best to respect your partner's decision and focus on changing your own accommodation, even if your partner is not going to go along. This is true whether you are two parents who are raising a child together, or if you are two parents who are not together, and you are each doing the job of raising your child separately.

If you decide it is best to focus on your own behavior for now and have accepted that you must go it alone, you can still be respectful of your partner. Your decision does not have to be confrontational or argumentative. You can let your partner know what you are going to do, explain your reasons, and accept that they can choose to disagree. The important thing is that the changes you make can still improve your child's anxiety, even if her other parent sees things differently and continues to respond to her anxiety in a different manner. Let your child know in your message that your plan only applies to you, without offering an opinion about what your partner is doing and whether that is good or bad. Then try your best to stick to your plan. Your partner may realize that your plan is helping and could change their mind. Or they may continue to act differently. Either way, if you are respectful of their decision and make a point of letting them know what you're doing without demanding they do the same, they, in turn, will be more likely to respect your opinion.

In This Chapter You Learned:

- How to improve communication with your partner
- What to do if you and your partner don't agree
- How to determine if there is a plan on which you can both agree

14

Wrapping Up and What's Next?

You Did It!

Parenting can be hard and parenting an anxious child can be extra hard. If you've worked through this book and followed the various suggestions for how to recognize accommodations while being supportive (rather than protective or demanding), and crafting and implementing plans for reducing the accommodation, then . . . well done!! I admire you, and I mean this in the most genuine and heartfelt way. I admire any parent who is determined and devoted enough to their child to take the time and effort to work on helping that child live a happier and healthier life, less obstructed by anxiety and freer from the impairment that anxiety can cause.

I also hope that the steps outlined in this book have achieved their primary aim of making your child feel less anxious. Nobody can be (or should be) completely free of anxiety and the goal of the book is not to completely remove anxiety from your child's life. I also hope that you have come to recognize that your child's ability to cope with anxiety is actually very substantial and that your child has realized this as well. If she has, then the work you have done is a tremendous gift to her, a gift that will continue to improve her life for as long as she lives.

If you feel that your child's anxiety has partially improved, but that he is still coping with significant and impairing anxiety, consider some possible next steps. You may need to continue working to reduce your accommodation, by taking on additional targets and working through the steps of making a plan and gradually reducing accommodation in this new area. You also may want to consider trying additional treatments and strategies. Chapter 2 discusses in brief some of the most evidence-based treatments for childhood anxiety, including cognitive behavioral therapy (CBT) and psychiatric medication. Appendix B at the end of the book provides some useful resources for learning more about evidence-based treatments and for finding a skilled provider in your area. Consider meeting with a capable therapist or psychiatrist in your area to discuss the possibilities. Remember that CBT requires a level of engagement and motivation on the part of your child, so this treatment may not be for everyone, but if your child is open to at least exploring the possibility, he may find it to be very effective.

The same recommendations are applicable if you feel that the hard work you put into completing the method described in this book have not really had much of an impact on your child's anxiety. No treatment can be successful for all children and timing can be important. If working through this book has not helped, don't blame yourself or become frustrated or discouraged. It is likely that the changes you made have helped your child and will continue to do so, even if at the moment it seems like not much has changed. Knowing you accept and believe in your child is important and impactful, even when anxiety levels remain high.

Keep Up the Support

If your child's anxiety has improved and things are returning to a more routine pattern without the need for special plans to help your child cope, it is important to keep up the supportive attitude toward her anxiety. You will probably face many situations in which your child struggles with one challenge or another. Some of these challenges will be anxiety-related, others will not be, and a supportive attitude will be helpful in most. Showing your child that you can accept and validate what she is feeling, while also demonstrating confidence in her ability to handle challenges and tolerate some discomfort will rarely go wrong.

For anxiety-related challenges in particular, a supportive attitude expressed in your words and your actions, can help to prevent future anxiety from escalating or growing to a point where it is again a major problem. Using the supportive statements you practiced during this process will also serve as a signal to your child, reminding him of the need to cope independently and reducing the risk of you falling back into less helpful accommodations.

Remember that children with a tendency or predisposition to elevated anxiety are likely to experience greater than typical anxiety many times over the course of their lives. You will have your own "family-language" for talking about the anxiety and for how to cope with it, so stay on the lookout for signs that your child's anxiety is growing, and be prepared to meet it in a supportive way. Periods of elevated family stress, transitions such as moving to a new home or school, losses that occur in a child's life, and social stressors can all contribute to increased anxiety, even after it has been successfully treated. Other times a child's anxiety will seem to grow even without a particular stressor or trigger. No matter the reason, if your child's anxiety seems to be coming back, a supportive parental response is likely to be helpful.

Notice Your Accommodation

By now you're an accommodation expert! That's great because it will make it easier for you to notice if you are falling back into old patterns of accommodation, or starting to develop new ones. Even parents who know a lot about accommodation and anxiety can sometimes find themselves suddenly realizing they have taken on some new accommodation. It can happen easily, and sometimes it takes a while to realize it. If you do notice that you are beginning to accommodate more, you know what to do! Don't get frustrated! Instead, be supportive, focus on your own behavior, and reduce the accommodation.

It never helps to get angry at a child for being anxious, and it doesn't make a lot of sense to do so, but you've worked so hard at helping your child get less anxious that it's natural if you feel a little exasperated when you realize the old patterns are creeping back. But stay positive. Chances are that if you've successfully reduced your accommodation and your child's anxiety once, then doing so again will be considerably easier. The supportive statements and accommodation plans will be much more familiar to both you and your child, and not quite as daunting. And you'll have something you couldn't have the first time: You'll have the knowledge that doing it in the past worked! Your child still may be frustrated if you don't accommodate, but he also will know that you helped him this way in the past, and that when you make a plan you can stick to it.

A great tool for noticing "accommodation relapse" is a monthly check-in. You can use the worksheets from this book to quickly survey your routine every few weeks and take stock of any new or lingering accommodations. You can do a check-in on your own, with a partner, or with your child. In fact, it's not only you who has become an accommodation expert. Your child has become one, too. Many children even point out to their parents when the children notice the parents beginning to accommodate. Sometimes this takes the form of an explicit statement, whereas other times it is more of a hint.

> Lila was 11 years old and her parents, Shirley and Terrence, had worked hard to reduce the accommodation of her anxiety. They had worked through two separate accommodation plans, one to stop screening movies ahead of time to make sure they did not include anything scary such as fires or floods, and the other to stop checking the local news whenever Lila heard a siren in the neighborhood. Their plans

had worked well, and Lila was much less anxious about disasters and catastrophes.

A few months after things had returned to normal, and during which Lila had only infrequently seemed highly anxious, Lila returned from school very upset. A classmate had told the class a frightening story about her grandmother's home being flooded in a major storm and had described in vivid detail how her grandmother had almost died in the flood. Lila told Shirley about the story and ended with: "I need you to check the weather channel and tell me if there is going to be a storm here as well. But you probably won't do that, will you?"

Shirley may have been feeling that checking the weather channel one time would not be such a big deal. After all, Lila has been doing so well, and is it really that bad to help her this one time, when she's clearly nervous and just heard a rather dramatic story? Perhaps checking one time would not hurt? It's possible that, in fact, it would not. But think about things from Lila's perspective. She is encountering her fears and worries for the first time in a while and is waiting to see how her mother will respond. The event is an opportunity to "help" Lila by checking the news. But it is also a very good opportunity to remind her of how strong and capable she is. By not checking the news, Shirley can remind her daughter that coping with anxiety is something that we all have to do sometimes and that she has full confidence that Lila can do just that.

Interestingly, what do you think about Lila's last sentence? It's possible to hear her words (*"you probably won't do that, will you?"*) as a frustrated or plaintive accusation that her mother won't help her. Another way to hear the same words, however, is as a statement of knowledge and strength, in which Lila may be saying to her mother, "We both know that is not really what I need right now." In fact, it's quite possible that if Shirley did check the news for her, Lila would feel let down and disappointed, rather than pleased. She would probably be relieved to learn there are no major storms on the way, but she could also feel disappointed that her mother was not sticking to the supportive message of strength and confidence. And importantly, Lila would be more likely to feel anxious again soon and to seek more accommodation from her mother. If Shirley responds with a supportive statement, Lila may be less relieved, but she will know that her mother's confidence in her is not shaken by the return of some anxious thoughts and feelings.

For a child who has overcome anxiety and has been feeling less worried, the appearance of a new anxious thought can be just as discouraging as it can be for her parent. She may feel nervous about whether this means she is not really better and whether she is back to square one. A calm and supportive response that takes for granted that, of course, there are going to be more anxious moments can be very helpful in keeping things in perspective and stopping the anxiety from getting bigger.

Remember, you are always the mirror your child is looking into to see himself. You have done something any parent can aspire to do and feel proud of accomplishing: You've shown your child a view of himself as strong, capable, and loved. If your child gives you more and more opportunities to show him that view, well, that's not really a bad thing at all!

Appendix A

Worksheets

This appendix contains all of the worksheets mentioned in the book. Feel free to make additional copies of these as you may need more than one as you work through the book.

Worksheet Number	Worksheet Title	Chapter in Which the Worksheet Is Discussed
1	How Is Anxiety Impacting Your Child?	Chapter 1
2	Parenting Traps	Chapter 4
3	You and Your Child's Anxiety	Chapter 5
4	Accommodation List	Chapter 6
5	Accommodation Map	Chapter 6
6	Things You Say	Chapter 7
7	Supportive Statements	Chapter 7
8	Your Plan	Chapter 9
9	Announcement	Chapter 10
10	Monitoring Target Accommodation	Chapter 11

Worksheet 1
How Is Anxiety Impacting Your Child?

Use this worksheet to write down the main ways in which you've noticed anxiety impacting your child in each of the four domains: body, thoughts, feelings, and behaviors

How Anxiety Affects Your Child's Body	How Anxiety Affects Your Child's Thinking
e.g., Her heart races when she is anxious	*e.g., He always thinks of the worst-case scenario*

How Anxiety Affects Your Child's Feelings	How Anxiety Affects Your Child's Behavior
e.g., She is much crankier when she's anxious	*e.g., He won't speak in class at school*

Worksheet 2
Parenting Traps

Use this worksheet to write down some of the *Protective* or *Demanding* things you say to your child or about your child's anxiety.

Protective
e.g., We know it's too much for you
e.g., You don't handle stress well

Demanding
e.g., Try to act your age
e.g., It's not really that scary

Worksheet 3
You And Your Child's Anxiety

Writing down your answers to each of these questions will provide some useful information as you start to think about the ways you may be accommodating your child. If you live with a partner, it is a good idea to spend some time talking about this together.

How Much of Your Time Is Taken Over by Your Child's Anxiety?

What Are You Doing Differently for This Child, Compared to His/Her Siblings?

What Would You Do Differently if Your Child Was Not Anxious or Afraid?

Worksheet 4
Accommodation List

On this page, write down the accommodations you are aware of. Try to think of as many as possible, but don't worry if you leave some out!

How Do You Accommodate?

Worksheet 5
Accommodation Map

Use the Accommodation Map to write down all the accommodations that occur throughout the day. Use another page if you run out of space.

Time of Day	What Happens? Who Is Involved?	Frequency (Tally)
Morning (getting up, getting dressed, breakfast, going to school)	e.g., Mom serves breakfast with "special" dishes	1 X Day
Afternoon (lunch, pick up from school, homework, after-school activities, social activities)		
Evening (dinner, family time, pre-bedtime)		
Bedtime (getting ready for bed, washing up/showering, going to bed)		
Nighttime		
Weekend		

Worksheet 6
Things You Say

Use this worksheet to write down the things you say to your child when the child is anxious and note whether they include the two elements of support: *acceptance* and *confidence*

Things You Say	Acceptance	Confidence
e.g., You just have to power through		✓
e.g., I understand this is very difficult for you	✓	

Worksheet 7
Supportive Statements

Use this worksheet to change some of the things you usually say into supportive statements that include the two elements of support: *acceptance* and *confidence*

Old Statement	Acceptance	Confidence	New Statement	Acceptance	Confidence
e.g., You just have to power through		✓	It's hard, but you have the power to get through!	✓	✓
e.g., I understand this is very difficult for you	✓		I understand how hard it is for you, but I know you'll be ok	✓	✓

Worksheet 8
Your Plan

Use this worksheet to write down your plan for reducing accommodation. Include as much detail as possible about the What, When, Who, How, and How Much of your plan, and What you will do instead.

WHAT

_____

WHEN

_____

WHO

_____

HOW AND HOW MUCH

_____

WHAT YOU WILL DO INSTEAD

_____

Worksheet 9
Announcement

Use this worksheet to write down the message you will give your child informing him or her about your plan for reducing accommodation. The message should be brief, supportive, and specific and should include the *What, When, Who* and *How and How Much* of your plan.

You can make extra copies of this worksheet or, if you prefer, you can work on your computer instead.

Worksheet 10
Monitoring Target Accommodation

Use this worksheet to keep track of and monitor your progress in reducing the target accommodation. Write down the day and time of each opportunity to implement your plan and briefly describe what you did, how it went, and any difficulties you encountered. You can make extra copies of this worksheet or, if you prefer, you can work on your computer instead.

Day	Time	SITUATION: What happened? What did you do? How did it go? Any problems?

Appendix B

Resources

Many resources provide excellent information about childhood anxiety and obsessive-compulsive disorder. These include books, websites, and other tools to help find expert care. Below is a very partial list of these resources.

Books For Parents

Freeing Your Child From Anxiety: Practical Strategies to Overcome Fears, Worries, and Phobias and Be Prepared for Life—From Toddlers to Teens. Author: Tamar Chansky

Freeing Your Child From Obsessive-Compulsive Disorder. Author: Tamar Chansky

Anxiety Relief for Kids. Author: Bridget Flynn Walker

Helping Your Anxious Child. Authors: Ron Rapee, Ann Wignall, Susan Spence, Heidi Lyneham, Vanessa Cobham

Books for Children

What to Do When You Worry Too Much: A Kid's Guide to Overcoming Anxiety. Author: Dawn Huebner

Outsmarting Worry: An Older Kid's Guide to Managing Anxiety. Author: Dawn Huebner

The Anxiety Workbook for Teens. Author: Lisa Schab

Guts (a graphic novel about fear of throwing up). Author: Raina Telgemeier

Rewire Your Anxious Brain. Authors: Catherine Pittman and Elizabeth Karle

The Thought That Counts: A Firsthand Account of One Teenager's Experience with Obsessive-Compulsive Disorder. Author: Jared Kant, with Martin Franklin and Linda Wasmer Andrews

Websites with Information and Tools for Finding Expert Providers

Anxiety Disorders Association of America: www.adaa.org
International OCD Foundation: www.ocfoundation.org
Association for Behavioral and Cognitive Therapies: www.abct.org
The approach to reducing family accommodation described in this book is called SPACE. On this website you can find a list of therapists trained in providing SPACE to parents and participate in a forum for parents of anxious children: www.spacetreatment.net

Index

Tables and figures are indicated by *t* and *f* following the page number

For the benefit of digital users, indexed terms that span two pages (e.g., 52–53) may, on occasion, appear on only one of those pages.